THE HUTCHINSON ENCYCLOPEDIA

Family

QUIZ

Book 4

Helicon

Copyright © Helicon Publishing Ltd 1996

Helicon Publishing Ltd
42 Hythe Bridge Street
Oxford OX1 2EP

Printed and bound in Great Britain by
Cox & Wyman Ltd, Reading, Berkshire

ISBN 1-85986-196-2

British Cataloguing in Publication Data
A catalogue record for this book is available
from the British Library

THE HUTCHINSON ENCYCLOPEDIA

Family

QUIZ

Book 4

Quiz Numbers

Contributors

Christopher Gray
Ann Kelsall
Antony Moore
Benedict Ramos

Editors

Editorial Director
Hilary McGlynn

Project Editors
Clare Ramos
Avril Cridlan

Text Editor
Sam Merrell

Production
Tony Ballsdon

Page make-up
TechType

EASY

General Knowledge 1

1   Which country has special teahouses and an elaborate tea ceremony?

2   What kind of electricity can be produced by combing your hair?

3   Why did Edward VIII have to abdicate in 1936?

4   Where in your body would you find your epidermis?

5   What term is given to the points in spring and autumn when the Sun's path crosses the celestial equator, so that day and night are of approximately equal length?

6   Which rabbit was the hero of some of Beatrix Potter's stories?

7   Where were Geoffrey Chaucer's pilgrims going?

8   What nationality is the tennis player Boris Becker?

9   In which of the arts did Vaslav Nijinsky make his mark?

10   Which subject did Charles Lutwidge Dodgson, the author known as Lewis Carroll, teach at Oxford University?

Answers on page 159

Pioneers and Firsts

1   What was Yuri Gagarin the first man to do?

2   Who was the first man to reach the South Pole?

3   What kind of newspaper feature first appeared in the *New York World* in 1896?

4   Who was the Venetian traveller who visited the court of Kublai Khan?

5   Who invented both the electric light bulb and the phonograph?

6   Which seafaring explorer died of dysentery off Puerto Bello, Panama, in 1596?

7   What were the first names of the Wright brothers, who built the first aeroplane?

8   Which feat of endurance was first performed by Captain Matthew Webb in 1875?

9   Who was the first woman prime minister of Great Britain?

10 Who was the star of the first talking picture *The Jazz Singer*?

Answers on page 159

Colours 3

1   In a breathalyzer, the chemicals change colour to indicate the presence of what substance?

2   What colour rain did Prince sing about in 1984?

3   What colour are the flowers of flax, the plant which produces linen and linseed oil?

4   What is the name of the coloured part of the eye?

5   What colour is sulphur?

6   What colour are the stars on the flag of the United States of America?

7   What colour was the woad with which ancient Britons painted their bodies?

8   Who, in a musical, had an 'amazing technicolor dreamcoat'?

9   How many colours are there in a rainbow?

10 In the Bible which sea did Moses cross to reach the Promised Land?

Answers on page 159

First Names

4

1   What was the first name shared by the Pitts, father and son, who were both prime ministers of Britain?

2   What first name is also part of the surname of the man who became secretary general of the United Nations in 1992?

3   Neil walked on the moon, and Louis played the trumpet; what's their surname?

4   What first name is the title of a novel by Jane Austen?

5   What surname is shared by an actor called Roger, a sculptor called Henry, and a comedian called Dudley?

6   What name was the first name of the poet Shelley and the family name of Hotspur?

7   What was the first name of the father and son composers of both the Strauss and Bach families?

8   What was the surname of the brothers John, assassinated in 1963, and Robert, assassinated in 1968?

9   If Leonard was Chico and Arthur was Harpo, who was Julius?

10   What first name is shared by the footballer Cantona and the first European to find Greenland?

Answers on page 159

6

What's Up Doc?   5

1   What is the obvious symptom of jaundice?

2   What serious condition is treated with streptokinase and aspirin?

3   Where would you find a cornea and a retina?

4   What are you doing if you have rapid eye movement at night?

5   What do neurologists study?

6   What is the approximate weight in kilograms of the human liver?

7   How many ventricle chambers are there in the heart?

8   If someone has scurvy, what vitamin do they lack?

9   What radical technique was pioneered by Robert Edwards and Patrick Steptoe in 1978?

10 Which devastating disease is carried by fleas on Asian black rats?

Answers on page 159

1   Who was president of the USA at the beginning of the 1960s?

2   Which bad boys of rock recorded 'Satisfaction' in 1965?

3   Which tennis player is the only man to have won the Grand Slam twice, in 1962 and in 1969?

4   Which musical instrument was invented by Robert Moog in 1964?

5   Which cricketer hit six sixes in an over in 1968?

6   What was the title of Joseph Heller's 1961 satirical novel about war and bureaucracy?

7   On which island were the missiles that led to a confrontation between the USA and the USSR in 1962?

8   Who was the captain of the England football team which won the World Cup in 1966?

9   Of which country did Pierre Trudeau become prime minister in 1968?

10 Which city was divided by a wall built in 1961?

Answers on page 159

Kings and Princes

7

1   Who was the father of Henry VIII?

2   Which country's ruling dynasty from 1613 to 1917 was the Romanov family?

3   Who was emperor of Germany throughout World War I?

4   How did King Louis XVI of France die?

5   Of which country was Hamlet a prince?

6   Of which Caribbean island is Kingston the capital?

7   In which sport was Billie Jean King a champion?

8   How many kings called George has England had?

9   Which country's King Leopold III surrendered to the Germans in 1940?

10 What are the names of the two children of the Prince and Princess of Wales?

Answers on page 160

9

Mountains

1   Whose ship, according to legend, ended up on Mount Ararat?

2   On which mountain did Moses receive the Ten Commandments?

3   In which country would you find the Apennine mountains?

4   Which North American city is overlooked by Mount Royal?

5   What is the meaning of the name of the Swiss mountain the Jungfrau?

6   What is the second highest mountain in the world?

7   In which mountain range does the Missouri river rise?

8   In which mountain resort is the Cresta Run?

9   What is the name, from the Turkish for 'mountains', given to the peninsula that contains Albania, Croatia, Greece and the former Yogoslavia?

10   In which decade was Mount Everest first climbed?

Answers on page 160

1   Which two metals are used to make brass?

2   What does the periodic table list?

3   What material is used to make optical fibre?

4   How many arms does a starfish usually have?

5   What preserved Lindow Man from the Iron Age to 1984?

6   What is lignite used for?

7   What metal is used to make the element in a light bulb?

8   Who was the first person to fly solo across the Atlantic without stopping?

9   What metal can be extracted from malachite?

10   What is measured on the pH scale?

Answers on page 160

1   What is the correct title for an Oscar?

2   Who was called Hollywood's 'Love Goddess' in the 1940s?

3   What does the title of Hitler's book *Mein Kampf* mean?

4   What was the title of Emily Brontë's only novel?

5   What was the name of the union formed under the leadership of Lech Walesa in Poland in 1980?

6   What name was given both to the group who tried to seize power in China after Mao's death and to the founders of Britain's Social Democratic Party?

7   What is the name of the country home of the British prime minister?

8   What is the name of the Thursday before Easter?

9   What was the name of the vocal group made up of Diana Ross, Florence Ballard, and Mary Wilson?

10   What extra title has history given to Peter I and Catherine II of Russia, and to Frederick II of Prussia?

Answers on page 160

1   What radioactive gas occurs naturally in spring water, streams, and the air?

2   Which of the following metals is the most abundant in the Earth's crust: copper, iron, aluminium, or magnesium?

3   What gas is harmful at ground level but essential in the upper atmosphere?

4   Where is pumice stone produced?

5   What natural phenomenon produces morraine?

6   What gas do bacteria in the roots of peas and beans put back into the soil?

7   What blocks out the Moon in a lunar eclipse?

8   Approximately how many tonnes of sewage did Britain dump in the North Sea in 1987?

9   Where does geothermal energy come from?

10   Why did 684 people die in Minamata, Japan in the period 1953 to 1975?

Answers on page 160

1   Bobby Fischer become world champion of what in 1972?

2   Which 1977 film popularized disco dancing around the world?

3   What commodity's price rose tenfold during the 1970s because of the influence of OPEC?

4   In which country was Prince Juan Carlos de Bourbon crowned king in 1975?

5   What was the name of Andrew Lloyd Webber's 1978 musical about Eva Perón?

6   What title did the former King Edward VIII bear at the time of his death in 1972?

7   Who was the US vice president who resigned in 1973 after accusations of tax evasion?

8   What was the art exhibit *Equivalent VIII* by Carl Andre that caused an outcry in 1976?

9   What was the new name given to the city of Saigon in 1976?

10   Who was stripped of his knighthood in 1979 after being unmasked as a Soviet spy?

Answers on page 160

1   Which country has been ruled by Fidel Castro since 1959?

2   What invention did Georges de Mestral make when he noticed how burrs stuck to his trousers?

3   What was the name of the Dutch settlement on Manhattan 1624?

4   In basketball, how many players are on the court at any one time?

5   What geographical feature lies at the eastern end of England's South Downs?

6   What kind of creature is a hake?

7   What name did Alexander Calder give to his suspended shapes that move in the slightest breeze?

8   Which biblical character was hidden among bulrushes as a baby to save his life?

9   Who was lead singer of the Smiths?

10 Which race is the blue riband of the English horse-racing season?

Answers on page 161

Oceans, Seas, and Lakes 14

1   What is the main cause of tides?

2   On which sea does Beirut stand?

3   In which sea is the island of Corfu?

4   Which painter's seascapes included *The Fighting Téméraire*?

5   What is the biggest kind of shark?

6   Which body of water did Louis Blériot cross in an aeroplane on 25 July 1909?

7   Who was the Roman equivalent of Poseidon, the Greek god of the sea?

8   Which of the Seven Wonders of the World was useful to sailors?

9   Which country has coasts on both the Skagerrak and the Kattegat?

10   Where is a whale's blowhole?

Answers on page 161

Digging for Answers 15

1   In which country were the bones of the earliest known human ancestor, *Australopithecus ramidus*, found?

2   What was dug up at Sutton Hoo in 1939?

3   Which extinct animals are most closely related to birds and crocodiles?

4   Where did trilobites live?

5   What did Emperor Shi Huangdi have buried to guard his tomb?

6   Where were the bluestones used in the construction of Stonehenge from?

7   What happened to the Turin Shroud in 1988?

8   How many sides does a ziggurat have?

9   What kind of animal was an *Elephas primigenius*?

10   What huge dinosaur was discovered in 1995?

Answers on page 161

Colours in Nature 16

1 What colour is anthracite?

2 What colour is garnet?

3 What colour is the largest kangaroo?

4 What colour are the flowers of the herb tansy?

5 Which colour in the rainbow has the longest wavelength?

6 Describe the colouring of a killer whale.

7 What is the usual colour of topaz?

8 What colour are the flowers of shepherd's purse?

9 What colour is the element mercury?

10 What colour is the top of a green woodpecker's head?

Answers on page 161

1   With what gourmet food do you associate the town of Whitstable?

2   Which of these plants is not aquatic: watercress, water hyacinth, watermelon, water lily?

3   Which town is the centre of the champagne industry?

4   Which edible plant of the lily family was thought to keep away vampires?

5   Iran is one of the two main exporters of which delicacy from the Caspian Sea?

6   Which ingredient of tea and coffee is detrimental to health in excess?

7   Which bird produces the largest egg?

8   Which edible bird of the pheasant family is native to woodlands of the USA and Mexico?

9   From which country does Emmental cheese come?

10   A nectarine is a variety of which fruit?

Answers on page 161

Writers and Books 18

1 Who is the king in Tennyson's 'Idylls of the King'?

2 Who wrote the poem that begins 'I wandered lonely as a cloud'?

3 What was the title of Salman Rushdie's book that caused great offence to many Muslims?

4 Who wrote the *Just So Stories* and the poem 'If...'?

5 What was Johann Gutenberg's contribution to the world of books?

6 What is the name of the art of handwriting?

7 What kind of written record was superseded by the paged book in the second century AD?

8 What colour was the little book containing Chairman Mao's thoughts?

9 Who was the author of *The Chronicles of Narnia*?

10 Which statesman wrote *A History of the English-Speaking Peoples*?

Answers on page 162

1   On which plain is Stonehenge?

2   Which city in the USA was almost destroyed by an earthquake in 1906?

3   In which city, the second holiest in the Muslim world, is the Prophet's Mosque?

4   Which 14th-century castle was Paris' state prison until it was stormed by revolutionaries in 1789?

5   In which city is the Parthenon?

6   Which British cathedral was designed by Sir Christopher Wren?

7   Which countries are linked by the Simplon Tunnel, opened in 1906?

8   The 1,000-mile Grand Canal, the world's longest, is in which country?

9   Beneath which French landmark does France's 'Unknown Soldier' rest?

10   After which philanthropist was the Music Hall in New York renamed in 1898?

Answers on page 162

1   What is the SI unit of time?

2   How many times a day do devout Muslims pray towards Mecca?

3   Which French author wrote the series of novels called *Remembrance of Things Past*?

4   Who wrote the novel *Hard Times*?

5   What is the title of Stephen Hawking's best seller about time and the universe?

6   An isotope of which element is used for archaeological dating?

7   How many pips does the BBC broadcast to mark each hour?

8   Which year is the title of a George Orwell novel?

9   Whose early songs include 'The Times They Are A-Changin''

10   Which line of longitude does the International Date Line mainly follow?

Answers on page 162

1   Who took over the role of James Bond in the film *Live and Let Die*?

2   In which film did Sylvester Stallone make his name playing a boxer?

3   In the world of acting, what is Equity?

4   What was the nickname of Buster Keaton, the great comedian of the silent film era?

5   Why did Grace Kelly retire from acting in 1956?

6   Who directed his own performances in the title roles of the films *Hamlet* and *Henry V* in the 1940s?

7   Which actor starred in the films *Alfie* and *Educating Rita*?

8   In which film did Tom Hanks play a boy transformed into a grown man?

9   What were the first names of Laurel and Hardy?

10 Who progressed from acting, for example, in *Brighton Rock*, to directing films, such as *Gandhi*?

Answers on page 162

Animal Crackers 22

1   Which continent do aardvarks come from?

2   Which pink birds are called *Phoenicopterus ruber*?

3   What kind of animal is a grayling?

4   Which animal can close its nostrils to wallow in water?

5   What is the common name for beetles that produce light?

6   Which UK mammal eats insects and can roll itself into a ball?

7   Which is the largest seabird in the world?

8   What do kangaroos eat?

9   Which insects have queens, drones, and workers?

10 Which New Zealand bird cannot fly and locates its food by smell?

Answers on page 162

Discovery and Invention 23

1   What useful household device did Scot Hubert Cecil Booth invent in 1901?

2   What is the main raw material for making plastic?

3   In which year was the torpedo invented?

4   What did Daniel Fahrenheit invent in 1714?

5   What heat-retaining device was invented by James Dewar in 1872?

6   What is Quorn used for?

7   Who invented roll-film photography?

8   What single-rotor craft was first built in 1939 in the USA?

9   What was magnetic tape first used for in 1947?

10   What was the first plastic material, produced by Leo Baekeland in 1909?

Answers on page 162

Pairs

24

1   Who was Fred Astaire's dancing partner in *Top Hat* and *Swing Time*?

2   Who was Napoleon's wife from 1796 until 1809?

3   In which country did *Punch and Judy* originate?

4   Which other island forms a nation with Tobago?

5   Who wrote *HMS Pinafore* and *The Pirates of Penzance*?

6   Who wrote *A Tale of Two Cities*?

7   Who is Jayne Torvill's skating partner?

8   From which part of Adam's body was Eve created?

9   Whom did the impeccable manservant Jeeves attend?

10   Which other district of London is combined with Chelsea to form a borough?

Answers on page 163

26

1   In which field is Thomas Chippendale famous?

2   What is the second fastest swimming stroke?

3   Which Suffolk town is the centre of English horse racing?

4   Who did Ronald Reagan defeat in the 1980 US presidential election?

5   Who starred in *Butch Cassidy and the Sundance Kid* and *Out of Africa*?

6   What is another name for a donkey?

7   Who wrote the oratorio *Messiah*?

8   What nationality is the tennis player Ivan Lendl?

9   What is the name for the collection and study of postage stamps?

10   What is a spinet?

Answers on page 163

Islands 26

1 If Australia is classified as a continent, what is the biggest island in the world?

2 Who was the first known European visitor to Hawaii?

3 Which island stands at the southern entrance to the Bay of Naples?

4 Of which country is the island of Hokkaido a part?

5 Which great European city is built on piles on low-lying islands?

6 Where is Ellis Island?

7 On which Pacific island are there huge stone statues?

8 On which island are the Empire State Building and the World Trade Center?

9 About what kind of island did Robert Louis Stevenson write a novel?

10 Which island was the birthplace and inspiration for the singer Bob Marley?

Answers on page 163

1   For which country did Bob Geldof raise money in the mid-1980s?

2   Who became prime minister of Australia in 1983 and held office for the rest of the decade?

3   What popular name was given to President Reagan's Strategic Defense Initiative?

4   What was the name of the book by former intelligence agent Peter Wright that the British government tried to ban in 1987?

5   Whom did Prince Andrew marry in 1986?

6   Who lost the post of Chancellor of West Germany in 1982?

7   Who won an Academy Award in 1987 for his performance in the film *Wall Street*?

8   Whose 1985 album *Brothers in Arms* sold more than 20 million copies?

9   Where were the summer Olympic games held in 1988?

10 Which Australian film of 1986 was the most successful in the country's history?

Answers on page 163

1   In which field did Alessandro and Domenico Scarlatti make their names?

2   Which married couple appeared together in the husband's film *Henry V*, and the wife won an Oscar for *Howard's End*?

3   What was the first name of John F Kennedy's younger brother, whom he appointed attorney general?

4   Which great family of ancient Rome included the emperors Gaius Julius, Augustus, and Tiberius?

5   In which field were the Montgolfier brothers pioneers?

6   What is the name of the ruling house of Britain?

7   Which family of film stars included father Henry and daughter Jane?

8   In which country did Baby Doc Duvalier succeed his father Papa Doc as president?

9   What did the brothers Jacob and Wilhelm Grimm collect?

10   Which actor had actress daughters called Vanessa and Lynn?

Answers on page 163

Name the Year

1   In which year was the armistice signed that ended World War I?

2   In which year did Julius Caesar first invade Britain?

3   In which year was the Great Fire of London?

4   Which car was the first to be built solely by mass-production methods?

5   In which year did Yuri Gagarin become the first man in space?

6   In which year was Margaret Thatcher ousted as British prime minister?

7   In which year did Michael Jackson release the album *Bad*?

8   In which year did Prince Charles marry Princess Diana?

9   In which year was King Harold killed at the Battle of Hastings?

10   In which year was the soccer World Cup held in the USA?

Answers on page 164

Bits and Bytes

1   What is the smallest unit of information called in computing?

2   What is a WAN?

3   What software can replicate itself and transfer to other computers?

4   What does DOS stand for?

5   Which is the largest computer manufacturer in the world?

6   How does a modem connect to the Internet?

7   What does BASIC stand for?

8   What is the most powerful type of computer called?

9   What operates using lasers, ink-jets, or dot matrices?

10   Which of these is not an output device: monitor, printer, hard disk, or graph plotter?

Answers on page 164

Technology and Communication

31

1   Which red gems are used in lasers?

2   Who invented the telephone?

3   What is produced by the Haber process?

4   What communication system uses flags?

5   What popular means of communication makes use of a cathode-ray tube?

6   Which company produced the first personal stereo?

7   What does CD-ROM stand for?

8   Where would a flying shuttle be used?

9   What crystals are used to keep time in watches?

10 What form of communication did Johann Gutenberg improve in 1440?

Answers on page 164

1   What lies across the Danube from Buda?

2   Why was the Thames barrier built?

3   Who was the star of the films *Red River* and *Rio Bravo*?

4   On the borders of which two countries are the Niagara Falls?

5   At which city do the Blue Nile and the White Nile meet?

6   In which of the United States does the Mississippi reach the sea?

7   Which of the world's rivers carries the greatest volume of water?

8   Crossing which river has come to mean taking an irrevocable step?

9   On which river is the Henley Royal Regatta held?

10 Where would you find the Ponte Vecchio over the River Arno?

Answers on page 164

Early Scientists

1   In 1798, what did Benjamin Rumford notice produced heat?

2   French astronomer Leverrier predicted the existence of which planet?

3   What nationality was Pythagoras?

4   Where did physicist Fraunhofer discover dark lines in 1814?

5   What did the Greek philosopher Heraclitus propose was the force behind all change and motion in the cosmos?

6   Who invented the first electric cell?

7   Which Italian painter and scientist of the Renaissance studied anatomy and aerodynamics?

8   What form of sea transport was invented by Cornelius Drebbel in 1620?

9   What device did Isaac Merit Singer invent?

10   What did William Gilbert discover about the Earth?

Answers on page 164

Heroes and Villains

1   Which detective is the hero of Arthur Conan Doyle's novel *The Sign of Four*?

2   Which heroic figure supposedly held court at Tintagel?

3   What is the number of the spy James Bond?

4   Who was the gladiator who led a revolt of slaves against the Romans?

5   Which mythical hero performed 12 labours, including cleaning the Augean stables?

6   For what cause did John Brown, immortalized in the song 'John Brown's Body', fight?

7   Which member of Captain Scott's Antarctic expedition walked out into a blizzard so as not to delay his comrades?

8   Which biblical hero lost his strength when Delilah cut off his hair?

9   What was distinctive about the garb of the Australian robber Ned Kelly?

10   Which film hero encountered a Temple of Doom and made a Last Crusade?

Answers on page 164

Money   35

1   What is one hundredth of a dollar called?

2   Which European country has an economy largely
     dependent on gambling?

3   What phrase describes a country where taxes are much
     lower than elsewhere?

4   Who starred as the 'Man with No Name' in *A Fistful
     of Dollars*?

5   Which merchant bank collapsed in 1995 because of
     debts run up by a single trader?

6   What economic policy was advocated by Milton
     Friedman?

7   Which businessman died at sea in 1991 leaving an
     empire with debts of nearly 4 billion?

8   What does VAT stand for?

9   What was Judas' price for betraying Jesus?

10   Where is the US gold depository in Kentucky?

Answers on page 165

Plant Posers 36

1 What kind of food is traditionally sniffed out by dogs and pigs?

2 What do we get from cane and beet?

3 Which European tree lives the longest, sometimes up to 1,000 years?

4 Which grain is used to make Scotch whisky?

5 Which of these does not grow underground: peanut, cashew nut, sweet potato, or potato?

6 What is used to make oil, milk, tofu, and textured vegetable protein?

7 What is the common name for *Sequoiadendron giganteum*, the world's tallest tree?

8 Which tree produces acorns?

9 Which plant symbolizes St Patrick's Day?

10 From what part of a plant is natural cork made?

Answers on page 165

1   What is a frog called before it grows legs?

2   What do you get if you cross an ass with a horse?

3   Where do earwigs lay their eggs?

4   What animal's young are called leverets?

5   What is a baby lion called?

6   Which one of these lays eggs: scorpion, sea lion, dolphin, or sea horse?

7   What is a family group of killer whales called?

8   What is a young eel called?

9   Which animal's newly hatched young are called alevins?

10 Where do koala bear babies live?

Answers on page 165

1   What does the kelvin scale measure?

2   In which sport did Mark Spitz excel until his retirement in 1972?

3   Who was the famous husband of Anne Hathaway?

4   With which musical instrument is Mstislav Rostropovich associated?

5   Which game did YMCA instructor Dr James Naismith invent in 1891?

6   What are Leghorns, Rhode Island Reds, and Jersey White Giants?

7   What title did Adolf Hitler adopt as leader of the Nazi Party?

8   In which area of industry were Richard Arkwright's inventions primarily used?

9   What is the state capital of Oklahoma?

10   How is the result of a Papal election announced from the Vatican Palace?

Answers on page 165

Queens and Princesses 39

1   Which queen of England was the daughter of Anne Boleyn?

2   Which classic children's story includes the Queen of Hearts?

3   Which queen of Sparta was, according to legend, the most beautiful of women?

4   What title was given to Princess Anne in 1987?

5   In ancient times, where was Nefertiti a queen?

6   Which princess is the younger daughter of Prince Andrew?

7   In which of Shakespeare's plays is the title character encouraged by his wife to kill the king and seize the throne?

8   In the Bible, which king married Bathsheba?

9   Which queen had a house built at Balmoral to her husband's designs?

10   What was the nickname of Queen Mary I of England?

Answers on page 165

1   What is the colour of a novice's belt in judo?

2   In which battle did Davy Crockett die?

3   What is novelist Mary Shelley's best-known work of horror?

4   What was used for the first time at the Battle of the Somme?

5   Which screen Dracula later starred in the James Bond adventure *The Man with the Golden Gun*?

6   Which ground-dwelling bird of the cuckoo family is capable of running at 24 kph?

7   Which House fell in the title of Edgar Allen Poe's horror story?

8   What kind of fighting was outlawed in Britain in 1819?

9   Who was world heavyweight boxing champion from 1974–78?

10   How long is a round in professional boxing?

Answers on page 165

1   In which city in the Netherlands was a treaty on
     European union agreed in 1991?

2   Who became vice president of the United States of
     America in 1993?

3   Who came second to John Major in Britain's 1990
     Conservative Party leadership election?

4   Which 1990s rock group contains the brothers Noel
     and Liam Gallagher?

5   Who won an Oscar for his portrayal of an AIDS victim
     in *Philadelphia*?

6   In which country was Terry Waite held as a hostage
     until his release in November 1991?

7   To what office did George Carey succeed in 1991?

8   Which country was devastated by a civil war between
     Tutsi and Hutu in 1994?

9   Who directed the films *Reservoir Dogs* and *Pulp
     Fiction*?

10   Which astronomer's name was given to the space
     telescope launched by the space shuttle in April 1990?

Answers on page 166

Wars and Battles

1   On the site of which battle did Abraham Lincoln make a famous speech in 1863?

2   Which battle gave its name to an athletic event?

3   Against whom did Hereward the Wake lead a revolt?

4   In which modern English county did William the Conqueror defeat Harold?

5   In which war is Tolstoy's *War and Peace* set?

6   Where, according to the New Testament, will the battle at the end of the world take place?

7   In which country is Cape Trafalgar, off which the Battle of Trafalgar took place in 1805?

8   World War II started when Germany invaded which country?

9   Which weapon was invented by H S Maxim?

10   Which war is the setting for Hemingway's novel *For Whom the Bell Tolls*?

Answers on page 166

1   Where is the pituitary gland?

2   What fluid makes up 70% of human body weight?

3   Which is the largest tendon in the human body?

4   What organ has the oesophagus as an entrance and the duodenum as an exit?

5   What is the medical name for the skull?

6   What kind of protein are nails made of?

7   What is transported through the alimentary canal?

8   How many weeks does the average pregnancy last?

9   What is the function of the olfactory cells?

10 How many vertebrae are there in the spine?

Answers on page 166

1   Against which people does Astérix the Gaul constantly fight?

2   What was the name of the first theme park, opened by Walt Disney in 1955?

3   Which bells feature in the legend of Dick Whittington?

4   Which composer toured widely as a child prodigy in the 1760s?

5   Which dramatic actress made her name as a teenager in the films *Taxi Driver* and *Bugsy Malone*?

6   What was the name of the little lord created by Frances Hodgson Burnett?

7   Which frog was a star of *The Muppet Show*?

8   What organization provides cheap overnight accommodation for young people on active holidays?

9   What is the title of Laurie Lee's autobiographical novel about his childhood?

10 At a school in which city did the members of U2 meet?

Answers on page 166

1   What colour were the bricks on the road to the City of Emeralds in *The Wonderful Wizard of Oz*?

2   What colour is the cloth on a billiards table?

3   What colour are mistletoe berries?

4   Which sport has several carefully tended areas called greens?

5   What colour are the blood cells that can engulf bacteria?

6   What colour was the submarine in the animated film based on a Beatles song?

7   What colour belt is worn by the finest exponents of judo?

8   What colour is a male mallard's head?

9   What colour is a ruby?

10   In snooker, which colour ball scores five?

Answers on page 166

1   Who discovered the effects of laughing gas and invented the safety lamp?

2   Which naturalist, who worked with lions in Kenya, was murdered in 1985?

3   What theory did the physicist Schrödinger put forward?

4   What did Sydney Brenner and François Jacob discover in 1960?

5   Which vitamin did Charles King isolate in 1932?

6   Who wrote *On the Origin of Species*?

7   What nationality was the inventor of the telephone?

8   James Brindley was a builder of what form of transport?

9   Who built the Clifton Suspension Bridge?

10   Who discovered that microorganisms cause fermentation?

Answers on page 166

Trains, Planes, and Automobiles 47

1 Which year was the Channel Tunnel officially opened?

2 What were the first bicycle frames made of?

3 What vehicle glides across water on a cushion of air?

4 What are the *Ark Royal*, *Eisenhower*, and *Invincible*?

5 What name is commonly given to an aeroplane flight recorder?

6 In which city was the first underground electric railway?

7 How were Viking ships powered?

8 What gas do modern airships contain?

9 What was special about Brunel's ship the *Great Britain* built in 1845?

10 Which country's trains hold the rail-speed record of 515 kph?

Answers on page 167

1   After their secret marriage in 1846 where did Robert
    and Elizabeth Barrett Browning go to live?

2   Who composed the opera *The Marriage of Figaro*?

3   How many times had Wallis Simpson been married
    before her marriage to the Duke of Windsor in 1937?

4   Ted Hughes was once married to which fellow poet?

5   Of Henry VIII's six wives which ones did he divorce?

6   Which fellow Hollywood star did Mary Pickford
    marry in 1920?

7   Which American screen actress starred in *How to
    Marry a Millionaire* in 1953 and *The Seven Year Itch
    in 1955*?

8   Which Flemish artist painted the *Arnolfini Wedding* in
    1434?

9   Who played the estranged husband and wife in the
    1979 film *Kramer vs Kramer*?

10 Which Christian sect, whose headquarters are in the
    US state of Utah, officially practised polygamy until
    1890?

Answers on page 167

1   What does the mathematical symbol consisting of a horizontal line with one dot above and one dot below mean?

2   In the Wars of the Roses, which colour rose was the badge of the House of Lancaster?

3   In Roman numerals, what number does D symbolize?

4   What part of a greenshank is green?

5   Which sign of the zodiac is represented as the scales of justice?

6   What is the name of the computer-readable pattern used on grocery and books?

7   How did King Canute show his flattering courtiers that he was not all powerful?

8   What is the name of the mark made on gold, silver, or platinum to prevent fraud?

9   What is the word for signs of an illness described by the patient?

10 What colour does litmus paper go to show that it is in an acid?

Answers on page 167

Space: the Final Frontier 50

1   What orbits the Earth every 27 days at a distance of 384,000 kilometres?

2   In which year did the first man step on to the Moon?

3   What is our galaxy called?

4   Who proposed the general theory of relativity?

5   Which planet takes the longest to orbit the Sun?

6   Which country launched the first satellite?

7   What object in space has such a strong gravity that nothing can escape from it?

8   Which space probe took photographs of Saturn's rings in 1980?

9   Who said 'God does not play dice with the universe'?

10   Who invented the astronomical telescope?

Answers on page 167

MEDIUM

1   What do you call a triangle with more than one obtuse angle?

2   Which Spanish city gave its name to the oranges used in marmalade?

3   In which country are the Khmer the largest ethnic group?

4   Who was US president Gerald Ford's running mate in 1976, who has attempted to gain the Republican presidential nomination in 1980, 1988, and 1996?

5   Which country lies on the southern border of Belarus?

6   Who said that he got fed up with all the sex and sleaze of rock 'n' roll, so he went into politics?

7   Who or what is *Candida albicans*?

8   Who wrote the hit musical comedy *The Gay Divorcee* in 1932?

9   For what crime was Al Capone imprisoned?

10 Which novelist described her subject matter as 'Three or four families in a Country Village'?

Answers on page 167

1   In which country did settlers make the Great Trek?

2   In what field was Werner von Braun a pioneer?

3   What was Rowland Hill's postal invention?

4   Which conductor started the London Promenade concerts?

5   Which international organization was founded in Geneva in 1864 at the instigation of Jean Henri Dunant?

6   What did Martin Frobisher, William Baffin, and John Franklin all search for?

7   In which field has the American Ted Turner been a pioneer since 1980?

8   What style of painting was pioneered by Roy Lichtenstein, Andy Warhol, and Peter Blake?

9   Who wrote *Journey to the Centre of the Earth*?

10   Frances Cabrini was the first US citizen to become what?

Answers on page 168

1   What do the five coloured rings on the Olympic flag represent?

2   In astronomy, what colour shift in a star's light tells us that it is moving away from us?

3   What colour is the European shore crab?

4   The first Sherlock Holmes story was a 'study' in what colour?

5   What colour is a timber wolf?

6   What are the colours of the flag of the Netherlands?

7   What colour is the frill round the neck of a condor?

8   What is the Red Cross called in Muslim countries?

9   What colour were the shirts of Hitler's Storm Troops?

10   Which country's flag is simply a green rectangle?

Answers on page 168

1   What US president's surname was also the first name of the writer Capote?

2   Andrew was the first Johnson to become US president, but who was the second?

3   What were the first names of a Miss Parker and a Mr Barrow who were ambushed and shot by US police in 1934?

4   What was the middle name of the engineer Marc Brunel and the first name of his son?

5   What was the first name of Winston Churchill's father (who was also a politician)?

6   What nickname was given to Jean Baptiste Reinhardt, the jazz guitarist?

7   What was the middle name of the humorous poet Edmund Bentley, which he gave to a verse form that starts with the subject's name?

8   What is the first name shared by the first conqueror of Mount Everest and the English king known as Ironside?

9   What was the surname of the bank-robbing brothers Jesse and Frank?

10 In the Bible, who was the younger twin brother of the hairy Esau?

Answers on page 168

1   What disease is the drug zidovudine used to treat?

2   Addison's disease is caused by the failure of which glands?

3   What condition is caused by a person having an extra copy of chromosome 21?

4   What drug is in a placebo?

5   What is the common name for the drug acetylsalicylic acid?

6   What part of the body is affected in periodontal disease?

7   Which organ of the body is affected in glaucoma?

8   Which small animal carries the disease bilharzia?

9   What becomes inflamed in hepatitis?

10   Which part of the body is affected by impetigo?

Answers on page 168

1960s

1   Of which country did Constantine II succeed his father Paul I as king in 1964?

2   Which country became the first in the world to have a female prime minister in 1960?

3   What was the title of Stanley Kubrick's 1968 science fiction film?

4   Which African country unilaterally declared its independence in November 1965?

5   In China, what was the name of the mass movement directed against the upper middle classes from 1966 to 1969?

6   Why was Muhammad Ali stripped of his world boxing title in 1967?

7   What was the name of Kenneth Clark's 1969 television series about the history of art?

8   Which leader of the USSR was ousted from power in October 1964?

9   Which record producer was famous in the 1960s for his 'wall of sound'?

10 How did the Australian prime minister Harold Holt die in 1967?

Answers on page 168

1 Which king of England is supposed to have been murdered in the Tower of London on the orders of Richard III?

2 In which century was Charlemagne born?

3 Who has been the Greek king in exile since 1973?

4 Which European country restored the Bourbon family to its monarchy in 1975?

5 Which King wrote such horror novels as *Carrie*, *Christine*, and *The Shining*?

6 In which country is Prince Edward Island?

7 Of which European principality did Hans Adam II ascend the throne in 1989?

8 What is the family name of Prince Rainier of Monaco?

9 Who succeeded Henry VIII of England?

10 Of which country was Herod the Great king?

Answers on page 169

1   What is the name of the Buddhist kingdom high in the Himalayas?

2   Where would you find the core of an old mountain standing as an inselberg?

3   Which mountain was first climbed by Edward Whymper in 1865?

4   For what are Mount Palomar and Mount Wilson in California famous?

5   Which volcano in the USA erupted in 1980, devastating a vast area?

6   Where are the Southern Alps?

7   What is the name of the mountain range that stretches from Morocco through Algeria to Tunisia?

8   Which two countries are linked by the Brenner Pass?

9   Elbruz is the highest mountain in Europe; in which mountain range is it found?

10   On which continent are the Drakensberg mountains?

Answers on page 169

1   What drug comes from the *Papaver somniferum* plant?

2   What is the symbol for mercury in the periodic table?

3   Where would you observe the phenomenon of peristalsis?

4   What animal is a *Vulpes vulpes*?

5   What is stored in a capacitor?

6   What animal does the constellation Capricornus resemble?

7   What kind of animal is a mandrill?

8   What is a Solomon's seal?

9   What is a heliograph used for?

10 Which one of these fungi is safe to eat: cep, fly agaric, destroying angel, or panther cap?

Answers on page 169

1   What does Mussolini's title *Il Duce* mean in English?

2   Which British prime minister was known as 'the Great Commoner'?

3   What was the title of George VI before he came to the British throne?

4   What does the MI in MI5 and MI6 stand for?

5   Which golfer is known as the 'Golden Bear'?

6   What kind of machine might be described as VSTOL or HOTOL?

7   What is the short form of the name of Shropshire, by which it was officially known in the 1970s?

8   What was the name of the Argentine battle cruiser torpedoed by a British submarine during the Falklands War?

9   What name is given to an auction where goods are offered at a high price which is gradually lowered?

10 What was the nickname of General George Patton?

Answers on page 169

1   What does NERC stand for?

2   Which of these is not a fossil fuel: coal, natural gas, peat, or oil?

3   What do hydrologists study?

4   Which oil company was responsible for the massive oil spill in Alaska in 1989?

5   What is measured on the Beaufort scale?

6   How many people were killed by the explosion of the Chernobyl nuclear reactor?

7   What does HEP stand for?

8   What imaginary line encircles the Earth at latitude 66° 32´ North?

9   Approximately how many Javan rhinoceroses are there in the world?

10   What travels in aquifers?

Answers on page 170

1   Which country emerged as an independent nation
     under Sheik Mujibur Rahman in 1971?

2   Which building built on London's South Bank in
     1976–77 was designed by Sir Denys Lasdun?

3   What was the title of television naturalist David
     Attenborough's 1979 wildlife series?

4   Whose plays of the 1970s included *Jumpers*,
     Travesties, and *Dirty Linen*?

5   What was the former name of the oil company that
     became Exxon in 1972?

6   Which organization, formed in 1961, won the Nobel
     Peace Prize in 1977?

7   In which 1975 film did Jack Nicholson win his first
     Academy Award?

8   Who was elected president of France in 1974?

9   In which British city was there a terrorist bomb
     outrage in 1974 that led to six innocent men spending
     17 years in prison?

10   Who was appointed poet laureate in 1972?

Answers on page 170

1   From which part of a cow does brisket come?

2   What was the naval battle fought between Britain and
    Germany on 31 May 1916?

3   What is a chinook?

4   Who became the first footballer to score 100 goals in
    both Scottish and English football?

5   Which country has had ten kings called Christian?

6   What was the eventual fate of the Crystal Palace?

7   Why was an extra 385 yards added to the marathon at
    the 1908 Olympic Games?

8   Who was runner-up in the world motor-racing
    championship every year from 1955 to 1958?

9   Who holds the record for scoring most runs in first-
    class cricket?

10 In Morse code, what letter is represented by two dots?

Answers on page 170

Oceans, Seas, and Lakes   64

1   Which three countries lie on the shores of Lake Constance?

2   What is the name of the promontory of columnar basalt on the coast of Antrim, Northern Ireland?

3   What is the largest body of fresh water in the world?

4   What body of water separates Australia and New Zealand?

5   In which mountains would you find Lake Titicaca?

6   In which sea battle were the fleets of Antony and Cleopatra defeated in 31 BC?

7   Which ancient civilization invented the rudder and the magnetic compass?

8   On the shore of which gulf is the Ivory Coast?

9   What is the meaning of 'La Manche', the French name for the English Channel?

10   Who circumnavigated the world single-handed in *Gypsy Moth IV*?

Answers on page 170

1   Who wrote 'Lazy River' and 'In the Cool, Cool, Cool of the Evening'?

2   On what instrument is Ravi Shankar a virtuoso?

3   What is the other name for ska, precursor of reggae?

4   What popular musical style was associated with Lonnie Donegan?

5   Complete the Stephen Sondheim musical title *A Little...*

6   A sousaphone is a type of which brass instrument?

7   Which composer with the unusual first name Virgil wrote the music for the film *Louisiana Story*?

8   Who was the American jazz and blues singer known as 'the Empress of Blues'?

9   In which city did rap music first emerge in 1979?

10 Which record by the Platters was the first US number one hit in the doo-wop style?

Answers on page 171

Number Crunching

66

1   What distance would you have travelled if you went 5.88 trillion miles, or 9.46 trillion km?

2   What is measured in maxwell units?

3   What does the troy system measure?

4   What is a pascal the unit of?

5   What is measured in joules?

6   What are the units of electric current?

7   What are the units of power?

8   What is the measure of frequency?

9   How many zeros in a gigawatt?

10   What is measured in becquerels?

Answers on page 171

1   Who wrote the music for the ballet *The Rite of Spring*?

2   Which one of Shakespeare's plays opens with the line: 'Now is the winter of our discontent/Made glorious summer by this sun of York'?

3   Midsummer Day, 24 June, is the Christian festival of which saint?

4   How many seasons do the monsoon regions around the Indian Ocean have?

5   Where in Russia is the Winter Palace?

6   Which 18th-century Scottish poet, noted for his nature verse, wrote 'The Seasons'?

7   Which Italian artist painted *Primavera* (Spring) in 1478?

8   Paul Scofield appeared on stage and screen in Robert Bolt's play *A Man for all Seasons* as which 16th-century politician and author?

9   The Winter War of 1939–40 was fought between which two countries?

10   What is the common name of the plant *Colchicum autumnale*?

Answers on page 171

1   Who used his experiences in the British foreign service in his novel *The Spy Who Came in from the Cold*?

2   Which playwright unsuccessfully tried to reform the spelling of English?

3   What is the title of John Steinbeck's novel about migrant farm workers from the Oklahoma dust bowl?

4   In which country are Pearl S Buck's novels *East Wind-West Wind* and *The Good Earth* set?

5   In Mark Twain's satirical novel, where did the Connecticut Yankee find himself?

6   Whose story was based on the real-life adventures of Alexander Selkirk?

7   In which country was Albert Camus born?

8   Who wrote an open letter called *J'accuse/I Accuse* to the French president about the Dreyfus affair?

9   Who won the Booker Prize for his novel *The Remains of the Day*?

10 What kind of novels did Dashiell Hammett write?

Answers on page 171

1   In which US state is the Yerkes Observatory, which houses the world's largest refracting telescope?

2   Which famous landmark stands on the Champs de Mars?

3   What type of building traditionally had a barbican and a bailey?

4   Where is the Chinese pagoda designed in 1761 by William Chambers?

5   The Colossus of Rhodes was a representation of which god?

6   Which building was erected in Hyde Park, London, in 1851 for the Great Exhibition?

7   How is the English style of Romanesque architecture usually described?

8   At which major art gallery did James Stirling build the Clore Gallery, opened in 1988?

9   What colour is the Taj Mahal?

10   The earliest example of what construction was erected by Ptolemy Soter in Alexandria about 300 BC

Answers on page 171

1   What kind of years were in the title of Ivor Novello's 1939 musical?

2   Which artist included limp watches in his paintings?

3   Which sign follows Cancer in the zodiac?

4   How long was the war fought between Israel and its neighbours in 1967?

5   How long were the economic plans introduced in the USSR in 1928?

6   Which playwright wrote a number of plays on the subject of time, including *An Inspector Calls*?

7   For how long did Andy Warhol say that in future everyone would be famous?

8   Which jazz band leader composed 'One O'Clock Jump'?

9   How often were 'penny dreadful' magazines for women published in the early 1900s?

10   Who was the male star of the film *High Noon*?

Answers on page 171

1   Who starred with Humphrey Bogart in *To Have and Have Not* and then married him?

2   Who directed Cary Grant in the films *Notorious*, *To Catch a Thief*, and *North by Northwest*?

3   For which film did Jodie Foster win her first Academy Award?

4   Which singer starred in the films *From Here to Eternity* and *Guys and Dolls*?

5   Who won an Academy Award in 1986 for the *Color of Money*, as the same character that he had played in *The Hustler* in 1961?

6   Which film star was himself the subject of a film directed by Richard Attenborough in 1992?

7   Which US president was shot by an actor?

8   Which actress and singer was the mother of Liza Minnelli?

9   Which actor directed *The Milagro Beanfield War*?

10   In which film did Marlon Brando play the leather-jacketed biker Johnny?

Answers on page 172

1   How many species of alligator are there?

2   What kind of animal is an abalone?

3   What type of animal is used to produce the red food dye cochineal?

4   Which of these animals is not a marsupial: wallaby, Tasmanian devil, racoon, or opossum?

5   Where do bandicoots make their homes?

6   In what environment do manatees live?

7   What is a roach?

8   Which arachnids were the first to adapt to life on land, produce live young, and can sting?

9   Which is the only mammal that lives as a parasite on other animals?

10   Which small black, grey, and white UK bird flicks its tail up and down when on the ground?

Answers on page 172

1   To which animal are we most closely related?

2   What is the Latin name of our species?

3   To the nearest 10,000, roughly how many years ago did Neanderthal man die out?

4   In which century did Darwin propose his theory of evolution?

5   What did the 40-foot long dinosaur Brachiosaurus eat?

6   Who wrote *The Blind Watchmaker*, explaining the modern theory of evolution?

7   In which geological era did modern *Homo sapiens* evolve?

8   Who stated that giraffes evolved long necks because they were always stretching them?

9   What nationality was Gregor Mendel, the founder of genetics?

10 Which evolved most recently: dinosaurs, birds, mammals, or plants?

Answers on page 172

1   Who was Louis Cristillo's comic companion?

2   Who was the female star of the film *Bonnie and Clyde*?

3   Who teamed up with composer Carl Davis to write *The Liverpool Oratorio*?

4   Who wrote the ballet *Daphnis and Chloë*?

5   In which book of the Bible is the destruction of Sodom and Gomorrah recorded?

6   Which city makes up the Twin Cities with Minneapolis?

7   What distinguishes Laurel and Hardy's feature films *Babes in Toyland*, *Way Out West*, and *Swiss Miss*?

8   Rudolf Nureyev's legendary partnership with Margot Fonteyn began after he defected to the West on a visit with the Kirov Ballet to which European capital?

9   Who was Kurt Weill's collaborator on *The Threepenny Opera*?

10 Triton and Nereid were thought to be the only two moons of which planet until the *Voyager 2* probe of 1989 discovered six more?

Answers on page 172

1 In which country is the town of Spa?

2 Who was the first heir to the English throne to marry an English partner after 1659?

3 Which valley boasts the lowest point in North America?

4 Which English general gave his name to a style of sleeve?

5 In which country is Semtex made?

6 In which field did Manuel de Falla make his mark?

7 Who invented shells containing lead bullets?

8 How did the Thracian gladiator Spartacus meet his death?

9 Who is the only sportsman to have had world titles on both two and four wheels?

10 Who was the leader of the Crazy Gang from 1931 to 1962?

Answers on page 172

1   What is the name of the island on which Tokyo stands?

2   Which is the largest island in the Pacific Ocean?

3   Of which European power was Madagascar a colony until 1960?

4   On which Isle did Hereward the Wake have his stronghold?

5   To which group of islands does Lanzarote belong?

6   In Greek myth, from which island was Icarus trying to escape by flying?

7   Which group of islands includes St Lucia, St Vincent, Barbados, and Martinique?

8   Which poet wrote 'The Lake Isle of Innisfree'?

9   Which Asian island state is separated from the mainland by the Strait of Johore?

10 On which island did the painter Paul Gauguin live from 1891 to 1901?

Answers on page 172

1   Who won Academy Awards for directing *Platoon* in 1986 and *Born on the 4th of July* in 1989?

2   In which Canadian city were the 1988 Winter Olympics held?

3   Who was president of South Africa from 1984 to 1989?

4   Who won the men's 1,500 metres at the 1984 Olympic Games?

5   Who took over the captaincy of the Australian cricket team in 1985?

6   Who became poet laureate in 1984?

7   Who played the title role in the 1981 film *Arthur*?

8   Whom did Constantin Chernenko succeed as Soviet leader in 1984?

9   Who won the Booker Prize in 1986 for the novel *The Old Devils*?

10   Whose 1986 recording of Vivaldi's *The Four Seasons* sold more than a million copies?

Answers on page 173

1   Who were the French father and son of the same name who wrote *The Three Musketeers* and *The Lady of the Camellias* respectively?

2   Who wrote *The Brothers Karamazov*?

3   What was the surname of the French brothers Auguste and Louis who made the first cinema films?

4   What was the surname of the two half-brothers who both led the British Conservative party in the 20th century?

5   Who was Henry VIII's first wife?

6   Which royal house ruled France from 1553 to 1792?

7   What family occasion is the second Sunday in May in the USA, Australia, and Canada, and the fourth Sunday of Lent in the UK?

8   What relation were the composers Johann and Richard Strauss?

9   What relation were US presidents William Henry Harrison and Benjamin Harrison?

10 Which ruler put his brothers on the thrones of Naples, Spain, Holland, and Westphalia?

Answers on page 173

1   In which year was John Paul I's 33-day reign as pope?

2   In which year were the two battles of El Alamein?

3   In which year did Black Thursday cause Wall Street to crash and start the Depression?

4   In which year was the Suez Crisis?

5   Which year saw the Prague Spring in Czechoslovakia and student uprisings in France?

6   In which year did Franklin Roosevelt die and Harry Truman succeed him as US president?

7   In which year did Brian Mulroney become prime minister of Canada, and Robert Muldoon stop being prime minister of New Zealand?

8   In which year did Ayatollah Khomeini call for Salman Rushdie to be killed?

9   In which year was Charles I beheaded?

10   In which year did Elvis Presley die?

Answers on page 173

1   Which of these is not a programming language: SQL, PASCAL, ESP, or LISP?

2   What are the dots that make up screen images called?

3   What crystal is used to make microchips?

4   What does WYSIWYG mean?

5   What is a GUI?

6   Which of these is not an input device: light pen, scanner, graphics tablet, or VDU?

7   Which US county is called Silicon Valley?

8   What are CP/M, MS-DOS, and Unix?

9   What does OCR stand for?

10   What does IBM stand for?

Answers on page 173

1   What public means of communication was established in 1635?

2   Which industry uses picas, points, plates, and photosetting?

3   What is hardened by the process of vulcanization?

4   What are Baskerville, Bembo, and Bookman examples of?

5   What medical imaging technique uses sound waves?

6   Which multinational food, drink, and detergent company was formed in 1930 in a merger of British and Dutch companies?

7   What is made using the Solvay process?

8   What rust-resistant alloy was first produced in the UK in 1913?

9   What is the common name for the waxlike chemical PTFE?

10   Between which two English cities was the first public telegraph line laid?

Answers on page 173

1   Why are the Angel Falls so named?

2   Which country's principal river is the Murray?

3   Which city, founded on 1 January 1502, is named after a non-existent river?

4   Which African river gives its name to two countries?

5   On which river was the liner *Queen Elizabeth* built?

6   Into which sea does the Volga flow?

7   Which river flows past Notre Dame cathedral in Paris?

8   What is the Severn bore?

9   What are oxbow lakes called in the Gulf States of the USA?

10 Which capital city stands on the river Tagus?

Answers on page 174

1   Which Greek physician proposed the theory of humours and blood circulation?

2   Which Italian astronomer proved that Venus was orbiting the Sun?

3   Which doctor founded the Royal College of Physicians in 1518?

4   Who first classified plants and gave them Latin names?

5   What disease bacteria did Robert Koch isolate in 1882?

6   Who stated in 1665 that the Earth exerts a constant force on falling bodies?

7   Which Greek philosopher classified numbers as either triangular or square?

8   Who proposed the corpuscular theory of light?

9   Who established the principle of buoyancy?

10 Who first studied anatomy?

Answers on page 174

1   In which American state was the Boeing company founded?

2   Which female aviator flew solo from London to Australia in 1930?

3   Who was the first American in space?

4   The use of which gas made airships vulnerable to fire?

5   Who in fiction teaches Wendy, John, and Michael Darling to fly?

6   Which manufacturer made the TriStar in the 1960s?

7   Which space shuttle orbiter was destroyed in a midair explosion in 1986?

8   What is the other name for a dunnock?

9   To which family of birds does the nightingale belong?

10   Which kind of flying machine did Otto Lilienthal and George Cayley help develop?

Answers on page 174

1   Which ancient civilization invented coins?

2   What term is used for the European Community rate
     for converting farm prices to sterling?

3   What coloured term is used for stocks that are strong,
     reliable, and secure?

4   What is the currency unit of the Republic of Ireland?

5   In which business did the Rockefellers make their
     millions?

6   Which ancient king of Lydia was famed for his
     wealth?

7   Which African country was once known as the Gold
     Coast?

8   Who, in the Bible, made a golden calf?

9   What is the kind of Israeli farm where property and
     earnings are collectively owned?

10   Which system of directly transferring payments from
     one bank or post-office account to another was
     introduced in Britain in 1968?

Answers on page 174

1   Which of these materials is not made from a plant: viscose, silk, cotton, or jute?

2   What type of plant is seaweed?

3   What blue-flowered plant is grown to make linen and linseed oil?

4   Which of these is not a tree: gingko, trefoil, lime, or hornbeam?

5   What is the common name of trees in the genus *Fagus*?

6   What family of plants do lupins belong to?

7   What part of the liquorice plant is dried as a spice?

8   What are the dried and fermented leaves of *Camellia sinensis* used for?

9   What orange-scented essence is obtained from the evergreen tree *Citrus bergamia*?

10   Which one of these is a plant: sea cucumber, sea lily, sea potato, or seakale?

Answers on page 174

1   How, according to Shakespeare, did Cleopatra kill herself?

2   Who played the scheming anti-heroine in the film *Dangerous Liaisons*?

3   Who requested the head of John the Baptist from her stepfather Herod Antipas?

4   Who was the star of *Dangerous*, *Jezebel*, and *All About Eve*?

5   Who murdered her husband Agamemnon?

6   Of which Italian city was Lucrezia Borgia the duchess from 1501 to her death in 1519?

7   Which star of *Double Indemnity* and other film dramas was born Lucy Stevens?

8   What was Ulrike Meinhof's job before she became a terrorist?

9   Lady Castlemaine, Lady Portsmouth, and Lucy Walter were mistresses of which English king?

10   In Greek mythology, who was the sea-nymph who waylaid Odysseus for seven years?

Answers on page 174

1   What is the highest speed it is theoretically possible
        for any object to attain?

2   What happens to sound when it gets hotter?

3   Which planet orbits the Sun once every 0.24 years?

4   How many days does it take for the Moon to go round
        the Earth?

5   What is the record time taken for a passenger sea
        vessel to cross the Atlantic?

6   How long did the first steamship take to cross the
        Atlantic?

7   What form of transport has a speed record of 515 kph/
        320 mph?

8   At approximately what rate does the human heart
        beat?

9   What bird can fly at 80 kph/50 mph, covering as much
        as 600 miles a day?

10   How fast can a cheetah run?

Answers on page 175

1   From the throne of which country did Queen Wilhelmina abdicate in 1948?

2   Who wrote *The Snow Queen*?

3   Which queen of Spain supported Christopher Columbus's voyages to the New World?

4   In which century did Catherine the Great rule Russia?

5   Who was the English colonist whose life was saved by the Indian princess Pocahontas?

6   Which actress played Elizabeth I in the 1971 television series *Elizabeth R*?

7   How long was Lady Jane Grey's reign?

8   Which kind of bee has the job of fertilizing the queen bee?

9   In the USA, what words do they sing to the same tune as 'God Save the Queen'?

10 Which Romantic poet wrote 'Queen Mab'?

Answers on page 175

1   What was the fasces, the Roman symbol of authority, which gave its name to fascism?

2   In which religion is the use of marijuana a sacrament?

3   What bird is used to symbolize a person who believes in military action rather than mediation?

4   What kind of clothes do members of the Ku Klux Klan wear?

5   What desert animal was the insignia of the British 8th Army fighting in North Africa in World War II?

6   Which Christian festival marks the descent of the Holy Spirit on the Apostles?

7   What Greek letter is used in mathematics to symbolize the ratio of a circle to its diameter?

8   What is the emblem of St Peter?

9   What was the emblem of the Free French during World War II?

10   What are the markings on the back of the species of rattlesnake that is the most dangerous snake in North America?

Answers on page 175

1   In which country did Jean Chrétien become prime minister in October 1993?

2   What job did Chris Patten take after his defeat in the 1992 British general election?

3   In which country did the death of Kim Il Sung bring his son Kim Jong Il to power in 1994?

4   Of which country was Edith Cresson prime minister from May 1991 to April 1992?

5   Who was the Israeli prime minister shot dead at a peace rally in 1995?

6   In which country does the 1991 Nobel prize winner Aung San Suu Kyi fight for human rights?

7   At which ground did footballer Eric Cantona attack a spectator in 1995?

8   Which breakaway republic was invaded by Russian forces in December 1994?

9   Of which city was David Dinkins mayor from 1990 to 1993?

10 To which country did president Clinton send 28,000 troops to lead an international relief effort in 1992?

Answers on page 175

1   Which country did Mussolini invade in 1935?

2   Who wrote the science fiction novel *The War of the Worlds*?

3   What is a Pyrrhic victory, named after the ancient King Pyrrhus?

4   During which war was Winston Churchill a war correspondent?

5   In which country were United Nations troops engaged in a war from 1950 to 1953?

6   Over what substance did Britain fight two wars against China in the mid-19th century?

7   On which peninsula was the Peninsular War of 1808–14 fought?

8   Who mounted the Tet Offensive?

9   The Arabs and Israelis fought the Yom Kippur War in 1973, but what is Yom Kippur?

10   Which two countries did Napoleon defeat at Austerlitz?

Answers on page 175

1   Where do you find synovial fluid?

2   What part of the body is bent in scoliosis?

3   Which of these is not found in men: prostate gland, Graafian follicle, maxilla, or breastbone?

4   When do women produce the hormone relaxin?

5   What is an erythrocyte commonly known as?

6   Which part of the body is enlarged in scrofula?

7   What is the common term for a naevus?

8   Where are the pectoral muscles?

9   What essential hormone is secreted by the islets of Langerhans in the pancreas?

10   Which part of the body is not working properly in someone on dialysis?

Answers on page 176

1   What was the aim of the Children's Crusade?

2   According to Peter Pan, what happens when a child says that they don't believe in fairies?

3   Which long-running cartoon strip is drawn by Charles M Schulz?

4   Who wrote about *The Hunting of the Snark*?

5   What was the nickname of the baseball player George Herman Ruth?

6   Which war did Rip Van Winkle miss by falling asleep for 20 years?

7   In the Bible, what was the young David's job when he killed Goliath?

8   What is the branch of the Girl Guides for those between 14 and 20?

9   What did the schoolboy William Webb Ellis invent in 1823?

10   Which romantic poet wrote *Childe Harold*?

Answers on page 176

1   In which Puccini opera did Nellie Melba and Enrico Caruso appear together in 1902?

2   Who wrote *Don Pasquale* and *La Favorite*?

3   W H Auden wrote the libretto for *The Rake's Progress*, but who was the composer?

4   Which celebrated tenor starred in the 1986 film version of *Otello*?

5   In which Italian city is La Scala opera house?

6   Who was Merry in the title of an operetta by Franz Lehár?

7   Richard Wagner's wife Cosima was the daughter of which famous composer?

8   Where did the first public opera house open in 1637?

9   The *galop* from which opera is the tune usually associated with the cancan?

10   Who directed the 1983 film version of *La Traviata?*

Answers on page 176

1   What did Telford and McAdam work to improve?

2   In which year did Florey and Chain discover penicillin?

3   Who demonstrated the rotation of the Earth in 1851?

4   In which subject did Dorothy Hodgkin win a Nobel prize?

5   Which US engineer designed the first successful steamship?

6   For improving which imaging technique did Richard R Ernst win the Nobel Prize for Chemistry in 1991?

7   Which archaeologist discovered the Mayan sites in Yucatán?

8   What subject did Fred Hoyle study and write about?

9   What theory did Thomas Huxley support?

10 What did physicist Brian Josephson win a Nobel prize for in 1973?

Answers on page 176

1   What was the main use for Zeppelins early in the 20th century?

2   What was Clive Sinclair's unsuccessful three-wheeled electric vehicle called?

3   What does TGV stand for?

4   Which year did the British and French tunnels under the Channel finally meet?

5   Why do some aeroplanes produce a sonic boom?

6   Which two cities did the first public railway connect?

7   Which year was the hovercraft invented?

8   What was the first nuclear-powered submarine called?

9   Who invented the pneumatic tyre?

10   What type of acid is in a car battery?

Answers on page 176

1   Which of these is not an insect: woodworm, silverfish, caddis fly, or tarantula?

2   What do aphids eat?

3   Where do caddis fly larvae live?

4   What insect might you find eating your library?

5   What is the common name for the red and black beetle of the Coccinellidae family?

6   Which insect has no wings but can jump more than 100 times its own height?

7   What does a click beetle do as it clicks?

8   Which of these is not an insecticide: pyrethrum, derris, malathion, or paraquat?

9   What do insects eat in the pupal stage?

10 Which insects build nests of soil up to 6 m high?

Answers on page 177

1   Which actor, famous for playing Western heroes, finally won an Oscar for *True Grit* in 1969?

2   In Shakespeare, who is the villain who persuades Othello that his wife is unfaithful?

3   Who was the heroine of *Gone With The Wind*?

4   What legendary lover was written about by Molière, Mozart, Byron, and Shaw?

5   In Hamlet, who kills Hamlet's father?

6   The name of which Norwegian politician, executed in 1945, became a generic word for a traitor?

7   Who was rescued by the Scottish heroine Flora Macdonald?

8   Who was the hero of Charles Dickens' most popular novel?

9   Who created the chivalrous loner Philip Marlowe?

10   Who was the leader of Hitler's brutal SS?

Answers on page 177

Space: the Final Frontier   100

1   What instrument was placed in orbit round the Earth by the space shuttle *Discovery* in 1990 ?

2   In which year was the first Soviet space shuttle launched?

3   Name the first space probe to hit the moon?

4   Which spacecraft flew past Venus in 1990 on its way to Jupiter?

5   Which planet is largest: Neptune, Mercury, Venus, or Saturn?

6   In which year was the planet Pluto discovered?

7   Who classified galaxies into types?

8   What object do Titan, Mimas, Enceladus, and Dione orbit?

9   What is the name of Pluto's moon?

10   Which year did Halley's comet last return?

Answers on page 177

HARD

1   Which Roman emperor was called 'the Apostate'?

2   What is the name of the African rodent that looks like a small kangaroo with a bushy tail?

3   After which London theatre were the farces of Ben Travers named?

4   What colour are owls' eggs?

5   In which state of the USA was the first atom bomb exploded?

6   In the Vietnam War, who or what was Agent Orange?

7   Who composed the opera *Pagliacci*?

8   In Greek mythology, what was the great skill of Arachne?

9   What engineer's name gives us an alternative name for the four-stroke cycle of an internal combustion engine?

10 What was the real first name of the jazz trumpeter Chet Baker?

Answers on page 177

1   In 1826, what was Joseph Nicéphore Niepce the first to do?

2   Whose pioneering voyage was completed by Juan Sebastian del Cano?

3   In which field were Charles Babbage and Alan Turing pioneers?

4   Of which musical instrument was the sackbut a precursor?

5   Which state of the USA is known as the First State?

6   Of which African river did Mungo Park trace the source?

7   On which ship did Darwin sail to South America as a naturalist?

8   What was the name of the space probe that flew past Jupiter, Saturn, Uranus, and Neptune in the 1980s?

9   Who invented the first solid-body electric guitar?

10   Who invented the geodesic dome?

Answers on page 177

1   Who was betrayed to the police by a mysterious 'Lady in Red'?

2   The colour of a crayfish is somewhere between which two colours?

3   What colour period followed Picasso's Blue Period?

4   What colour habits do Franciscan friars wear?

5   When processing orthochromatic film, what colour safelight should be used?

6   What is the more familiar name of the painting *Arrangement in Grey and Black*?

7   Which journalist's early work included *The Kandy-Kolored Tangerine-Flake Streamline Baby*?

8   What colour were the shoes in the title of Powell and Pressburger's 1948 film about a ballet dancer?

9   The flour of which cereal is used to make 'black' breads?

10   What were the colours of Fangio's Maserati racing car?

Answers on page 177

1   What was the first name shared by the painters Vermeer and van Eyck?

2   What was the surname of Napoleon's fanatical admirer Nicholas, which gave us a word for extreme patriotism?

3   What is the real first name of Pope John Paul II?

4   What were the first names of the film director D W Griffith?

5   What is the real first name of Woody Allen?

6   The man who gave his name to the parliamentary report Hansard shared a first name with which gospel writer?

7   What did the E stand for in Robert E Lee?

8   What is the first name of the Argentine president General Galtieri, who ordered the invasion of the Falkland Islands?

9   Miss Tandy won the 1989 Best Actress Oscar for *Driving Miss Daisy*, and Miss Lange won for *Blue Sky* in 1994; what first name do they share?

10   What was Nell Gwyn's real first name?

Answers on page 178

1   What passes through the trachea?

2   What kind of infection makes the body secrete interferon?

3   What breakdown product of nitrogen compounds causes kidney stones?

4   What substance does the body produce an excess of in Cushing's syndrome?

5   In which disorder do *grand mal* and *petit mal* seizures occur?

6   What is the common name for malignant melanoma?

7   What activity may lead to decompression sickness?

8   Where is the carotid artery?

9   What is the liquid component of blood called?

10 What type of work may lead to silicosis?

Answers on page 178

1   Whose 1968 world long jump record stood until 1991?

2   In which city was Robert Kennedy assassinated in 1968?

3   Who wrote music for 'spaghetti Westerns' like *The Good, the Bad and the Ugly*?

4   From which country did Israeli agents abduct the Nazi war criminal Adolf Eichmann in 1960?

5   Which writer refused the Nobel Prize for Literature in 1964, but then changed his mind because he needed the money?

6   In which country did Dr Antonio Salazar step down as prime minister in 1968 after 40 years?

7   Which soul singer began a long succession of hits in the 1960s with 'Fingertips'?

8   What was the title of Ralph Nader's 1965 book that led to a greater emphasis on car safety?

9   In 1964, which was the first of the pirate radio stations set up off the shores of Britain?

10   Who was the former mayor of West Berlin who became chancellor of West Germany in 1969?

Answers on page 178

1   In which modern-day country was Prince Gautama Siddhartha, the Buddha, born?

2   Which country's last king, Michael, abdicated in 1946?

3   Who was the king of Saudi Arabia assassinated in 1975?

4   Of which country was William King prime minister for 22 years?

5   Which disease is known as the king's evil?

6   In which century did the real-life Macbeth reign over Scotland?

7   Which African nation achieved independence in 1966 as a kingdom ruled by Moshoeshoe II?

8   Which king of Ireland was killed in battle against the Norse at Clontarf?

9   Which prince was defeated by Oliver Cromwell at the battles of Marston Moor and Naseby?

10   Which name of several French kings attracted the nicknames 'the Bald', 'the Simple', 'the Fair', 'the Wise', and 'the Mad'?

Answers on page 178

1   In which three countries is the Karakoram range of mountains?

2   What name is given to the style of mountaineering that uses Sherpas, fixed ropes, and oxygen?

3   In the Andes, what is known as *puna*?

4   Who won an Academy Award for directing *The Treasure of the Sierra Madre*?

5   In which country would you find the Sierra Madre?

6   Where is the Great Dividing Range?

7   In which US national park is Half Dome Mountain?

8   What is the Welsh word for a corrie, a hollow formed by a glacier?

9   Through which mountain range does the Salang Tunnel pass?

10   On which island is the mountain Adam's Peak?

Answers on page 178

1   What is the aphid pesticide pyrethrum made from?

2   What is the technical name for mares' tails clouds?

3   What is the common name of pyrite?

4   What is extracted from cinnabar?

5   What do Yemenis do with qat leaves?

6   In which year was oil discovered beneath the North Sea?

7   What are the chemical building blocks of cellulose?

8   What carnivorous animal has up to 200 legs and lives in the dark?

9   How many legs does a crab have?

10 What is a beta particle made of?

Answers on page 178

1 What is the title of the head of state of Kuwait?

2 What title did Queen Anne give John Churchill when she came to the throne?

3 What name was popularly given to the act that allowed the government to release suffragettes on hunger strike, and then re-arrest them?

4 What name was given to the French composers Auric, Durey, Honegger, Milhaud, Poulenc, and Tailleferre?

5 What was the name of the theatre in Dublin that staged the works of W B Yeats, J M Synge, and Lady Gregory?

6 Which state of the USA is known as the Show Me State?

7 What is the name of the two-wheeled vehicle in which the driver sits in harness racing?

8 After which French soldier was the group of American airmen fighting for France in World War I named?

9 What is the name of the Canadian part of Niagara Falls?

10 What did Thomas Newcomen call the early steam engine that he invented?

Answers on page 179

1   What do radiometric techniques tell us the age of?

2   What name is given to the uppermost part of the celestial horizon?

3   What kind of rock is the Giant's Causeway in Northern Ireland made of?

4   Where does the warm ocean surge called *El Niño* occur?

5   On what line is the attraction of the Earth's magnetic poles equal?

6   What value on the Beaufort scale makes a wind a hurricane?

7   What causes Dutch elm disease?

8   What is the average depth of the world's oceans in metres?

9   What effect causes water to go down the plughole clockwise in Britain but anticlockwise in Australia?

10   Approximately what percentage of the Earth's atmosphere is made of hydrogen?

Answers on page 179

1   Which Argentine dictator returned in 1973 to assume the presidency after 15 years in exile?

2   René Goscinny, who died in 1977, was co-creator of which cartoon character?

3   Which novelist wrote the 1976 best seller *Ragtime*?

4   Which of E M Forster's novels was published posthumously in 1971?

5   Which composer was appointed Master of the Queen's Music in 1975?

6   Which Canadian author published *The Diviners* in 1974?

7   Which aircraft manufacturer was implicated in a bribes scandal in 1974 that led to the fall of the Japanese prime minister?

8   Which actress, who had moved to Hollywood in the 1930s, returned to the screen in *Just a Gigolo* in 1978?

9   What phrase was coined in 1975 by the magazine *Harpers and Queen* to describe a style of cooking without rich sauces and emphasizing freshness and presentation?

10   Which computer language developed in the 1970s was popular in schools because of its turtle graphics?

Answers on page 179

1   Which country administers Christmas Island?

2   Which is the smallest of the 88 constellations?

3   What medal is given to US servicemen wounded in action?

4   What is depicted in the top left-hand corner of the Uruguayan flag?

5   Who was king of England in the year 1000?

6   Not counting the Children's Crusade, how many crusades were there?

7   For the hunting of which animal was the basset hound originally bred?

8   How many notes are there in a chromatic scale?

9   In mythology, who was carried off by Zeus when he took the form of a bull?

10   On which island did the technique of batik originate?

Answers on page 179

1   In which ocean are the Cape Verde islands?

2   What was the first name of the man after whom Hudson Bay was named?

3   What was the former name of Lake Malawi?

4   Which cold current from North America influences the extent of Arctic pack-ice?

5   What kind of sea creature is a *Hippocampus*?

6   What is the name of the sea between China and Korea?

7   What joins the Gulf of Mexico to the Caribbean Sea?

8   In which state is Australia's largest freshwater lake, the Great Lake?

9   Which explorer proved that no Arctic continent existed by drifting across trapped in the ice?

10   Which sea lies between Australia, New Guinea, and Vanuatu?

Answers on page 179

1   What is semiology or semiotics?

2   What, in music making, are crotala?

3   What kind of animal is a serval?

4   What is an armature?

5   What is taiga?

6   What sort of animal is a nematode?

7   What is a peridot?

8   What is a bhikku?

9   What is a mugwump?

10   What is a spinet?

Answers on page 179

My Other Job

1   Who interrupted a highly successful career as an author of detective stories to serve as a senior physician in a field hospital during the Boer War?

2   Which poet worked for a time as a bank clerk and then later as a publisher?

3   What did Polish pianist and composer Ignacy Jan Paderewski become in 1919?

4   Until his career as a double agent was made public in 1979, Anthony Blunt was a respected authority in which field?

5   What political post did Scottish writer John Buchan hold between 1934 and 1940?

6   What career did sailor Teodor Jozef Conrad Korzeniowski turn to when he left the merchant navy?

7   Which comic dramatist co-designed Blenheim Palace and Castle Howard with Nicholas Hawksmoor?

8   Which US tycoon became a Hollywood producer and designed and flew aircraft?

9   Which English novelist served for five years in the Burmese police force, an experience he reflected in his novel *Burmese Days*?

10 Revolutionary Che Guevara, writer Somerset Maugham, and cricketer W G Grace all received training in which profession?

Answers on page 180

1   To which family of plants does the herb caraway belong?

2   Which former cook to Tsar Alexander and the Prince Regent is recognized as the founder of *haute cuisine*?

3   In which two colours is the liqueur Chartreuse available?

4   What is injected into Roquefort, Gorgonzola, and Blue Stilton cheeses to produce the blue veins?

5   Which part of a tamarind tree is used as a flavouring?

6   When is the broaching day for Beaujolais, after which it may be drunk?

7   In the wild, which animals are responsible for pollinating bananas?

8   Under what variety of trees are truffles usually found?

9   What is carragheen moss?

10 With which race of people does the word 'chocolate' originate?

Answers on page 180

1   In what writing method were Timothy Bright, Thomas
     Shelton, Thomas Burney, and Isaac Pitman pioneers?

2   What was the name of the forgery that helped to topple
     the 1924 Labour government in Britain?

3   Whose poem 'The Dream of Gerontius' did Edward
     Elgar set to music?

4   Who played songs of love in the title of Oscar
     Hijuelos' 1990 Pulitzer prize-winning novel?

5   Which philosopher's teachings were published after
     his death as Analects?

6   In which city was the earliest known library?

7   Which film director wrote *Money into Light* about his
     experiences?

8   By which classic novel is Jean Rhys's *Wide Sargasso
     Sea* inspired?

9   Which civilization produced the *Book of the Dead*?

10   Who wrote of his experiences in Auschwitz in *If This
     is a Man*?

Answers on page 180

1   Who wrote *Institutes of the Christian Religion* in 1536?

2   Who first expounded the idea of lateral thinking?

3   Which Roman emperor made Christianity the religion of the empire?

4   Which word, originating in Polynesia, refers to practices prohibited because of religious or social pressures?

5   Whose 1961 novel set in World War II has a title which entered the language to express the dilemma of all false authoritarian language?

6   Widows of which religion formerly practised suttee by joining their husband's funeral pyre?

7   Which philosopher wrote his main work *Ethics* in 1677?

8   What is a chador, used by some Muslims and Hindus?

9   What are the followers of Zoroastrianism called?

10 In Medieval English folklore, what was the Land of Cockaigne?

Answers on page 180

1   What is the name of the two-day holiday that marks the start of the Jewish New Year?

2   What is the Seven Years' War called in North America?

3   Which is the only day of the week named after a goddess?

4   In which month do Christians celebrate Candlemas?

5   Which calendar has a year of only 354 days?

6   What kind of clock did the ancient Egyptians use to measure time at night?

7   Who wrote the oratorio *The Seasons*?

8   Which cathedral had the first public clock in England, which is still working today?

9   In geology, which period follows the Triassic?

10   Who wrote the play *Forty Years On*?

Answers on page 180

1   Which boxer did Robert De Niro play in the film
     Raging Bull?

2   What was Burt Lancaster before he became an actor?

3   Which part did Edith Evans memorably play in the
     film of *The Importance of Being Earnest*?

4   What was the name of the theatre company founded
     by Kenneth Branagh in 1987?

5   Which actress appeared in a play called *Sex* in 1926
     and a film called *Sextette* in 1977?

6   Which Victorian actor's real name was John
     Brodribb?

7   Which actor is thought to have been the first to play
     Hamlet, Othello, and King Lear?

8   Which US playwright has also acted in such films as
     The Right Stuff and *Steel Magnolias*?

9   Of which London theatre did David Garrick become a
     joint licensee in 1747?

10   Which actress had an amusing correspondence with
     George Bernard Shaw, who wrote the role of Eliza in
     Pygmalion for her?

Answers on page 181

1   What is the common name of *Mus musculus*?

2   Where does the musk ox live?

3   How do dolphins, bats, and whales locate objects?

4   Which type of insect makes up more than half of the animal kingdom?

5   Which of these is not a whale: dolphin, shark, porpoise, or finback whale?

6   What kind of animal is a manta?

7   Which seabird has a brightly coloured bill and lives in a hole?

8   What is the common name of the bird *Turdus merula*?

9   What kind of animal is a characin?

10 Which bear is the largest living land carnivore?

Answers on page 181

1   By what name is the 11th-century Spanish soldier
        Rodrigo Díaz de Bivar better known?

2   What was the pen name of the short-story writer H H
        Munro?

3   What was the adopted name of Russian revolutionary
        leader Lev Davidovitch Bronstein?

4   What is the stage name of English rock singer and
        songwriter Declan McManus?

5   What did California have which caused it to become
        known as the 'Golden State'?

6   Which British city was known during the 18th century
        as the 'Athens of the North' because of its wealth of
        intellectual talent?

7   What was the stage name of English-born, horror-film
        actor William Henry Pratt?

8   Which county's nickname is the 'Garden of England'?

9   What is the full name of Captain W E Johns' fictional
        flying ace 'Biggles'?

10   The head of which Roman Catholic religious order,
        founded in 1534, is known as the 'Black Pope'?

Answers on page 181

1   In which city was Romeo and Juliet's doomed passion played out?

2   Which monopoly was granted to composers Tallis and Byrd by Queen Elizabeth 1 in 1575?

3   Where would you see together the two symbols of a vertical line with six marks on it and a circle with a horizontal line through it?

4   What in classical mythology were Scylla and Charybdis?

5   Which card game for pairs was invented by the poet John Suckling?

6   Which 1961 film showed two young men in love with Jeanne Moreau?

7   What are Goldie and Isis?

8   The association between the poets Verlaine and Rimbaud ended in 1873 when Verlaine was sent to jail. For what crime?

9   Who in Greek mythology were the parents of Helen, the most beautiful of women?

10 About which couple did Samuel Barber write an opera in 1966?

Answers on page 181

1   What were the Celestial Police?

2   What prompted Cervantes to write a second part of *Don Quixote*?

3   Of which musical instrument is the bombardon a low-pitched version?

4   By what name is Robert McGregor better known?

5   What position did members of the Ashikaga and Tokugawa clans hold in Japanese history?

6   In which city has the Palio horse race been held annually since the Middle Ages?

7   What type of animal is a skink?

8   For what is the feminist Lucy Stone chiefly noted?

9   Where are all five classic Irish horse races run?

10   Who gave his name to America's smallest state capital?

Answers on page 181

1   Which European capital city stands on the islands of Zealand and Amager?

2   Why was the island of Tristan da Cunha in the news in 1961?

3   On which island would you find the palace of Knossos?

4   On which island is St John said to have written the Book of Revelation?

5   In which country is Robben Island prison?

6   Off which island did the new island of Surtsey rise from the sea in 1963?

7   Which is the largest of the islands of the Philippines?

8   Where would you find the islets of Langerhans?

9   In which group of islands is Bikini atoll, which gave its name to the bathing costume?

10   Which saint founded a monastery on Holy Island in 635?

Answers on page 181

1   Who wrote the plays *The Real Thing* in 1982 and *Hapgood* in 1988?

2   Which sport grew from 'Clunker' racing in California in the 1980s?

3   What firm's first outlet in Des Plaines, Illinois, became a museum in 1985?

4   Which format for sound recording was announced in 1987, with the first players reaching the UK in 1989?

5   Which boxer won world titles at junior-middleweight, middleweight, light-heavyweight and super-middleweight between 1980 and 1988?

6   Which Hollywood studio nearly collapsed after producing the disastrous *Heaven's Gate* in 1980?

7   What was the army rank of Samuel Doe, who scized power in Liberia in 1980?

8   Which female athlete won the London Marathon in 1984, 1985, 1987, and 1988?

9   Which city did the 1984 Olympic ice-dance champions Torvill and Dean come from?

10   Who wrote the 1980s trilogy of novels *Rites of Passage*, *Close Quarters*, and *Fire Down Below*?

Answers on page 182

1   What was the Christian name of British prime minister Alec Douglas-Home's playwright brother?

2   About which family did John Galsworthy write a saga?

3   Who wrote the poem *The Faerie Queene*?

4   The father painted *The Bathers* and *Umbrellas*, the son directed *The Rules of the Game* and *La Grande Illusion* – who were they?

5   What surname did actor Douglas Ulman take and pass on to his similarly swashbuckling son?

6   Who was the novelist grandson of the man known as 'Darwin's bulldog' for championing evolution?

7   What was the surname of the father and son, George and William, who both became British prime minister?

8   What was the surname of the father and son composers Alessandro and Domenico?

9   Which family of dukes holds the hereditary office of Earl Marshal?

10 What was the name of the Prussian ruling family who became emperors of Germany in 1871?

Answers on page 182

1   In which year did Humphrey Bogart star in *Casablanca*?

2   William Henry Harrison was president of the United States for only a month, but in which year?

3   In which year was the mutiny on HMS *Bounty*?

4   In which year did Charles Lindbergh become the first man to fly solo non-stop across the Atlantic?

5   In which year was Captain Cook killed in a skirmish in Hawaii?

6   In which year was Princess Grace of Monaco killed in a car crash?

7   In which year was the Eiffel Tower completed?

8   In which year did Marlborough defeat the French and Bavarians at Blenheim?

9   In which year did ex-president Theodore Roosevelt run again for the 'Bull Moose' Party?

10   In which year was the Islamic revolution in Iran that ousted the Shah?

Answers on page 182

1   Exactly how many kilobytes are there in a megabyte?

2   What does SQL stand for?

3   What was the first personal computer called?

4   Which year was Windows 3 launched?

5   What is the language PROLOG used for?

6   What does COBOL stand for?

7   What is used to translate high-level programs into machine code?

8   What does DIANE stand for?

9   What does MIDI stand for?

10   What are the units of speed of data transmission in computing?

Answers on page 182

1   What is produced by the Bessemer process?

2   What technique did Isaac Pitman use to write at 300 words per minute?

3   In which year did the BBC begin broadcasting TV programmes?

4   Where was the first telephone exchange?

5   In which year was the first transatlantic telephone cable laid?

6   What was the name of the US satellite which relayed the first live TV pictures between the USA and Europe?

7   How many lines are there in a television picture in the UK?

8   Where is the largest single-mirror reflector telescope?

9   Under which river was the first underwater tunnel built?

10   What do the letters FM on a radio stand for?

Answers on page 182

1   Which river joins the Ganges near Allahabad?

2   In which country is the river Menderes, which gives us the word meander?

3   Which three countries lie on the shores of Lake Victoria?

4   In which country is Cooper Creek?

5   What is the common name of the disease onchocerciasis?

6   Which river joins the Rhine at Duisburg?

7   In which country is the largest estuarine delta in the world?

8   Which country's longest river is the Bío-Bío?

9   On the bank of which river is the Valley of the Kings?

10   Who wrote the novel *The Bridge of Saint Luis Rey*?

Answers on page 183

1   Who first used a microscope to study the structure of plants?

2   Who proposed the atomic theory?

3   What did Johannes Müller discover *c*.1830?

4   What was Theophrastus studying in AD 300?

5   What animal eggs did Marcelle Malphigi use to study embryology?

6   Who discovered the link between nerves and electricity?

7   What did Christiaan Huygens invent in 1656?

8   Who related volumes and numbers of molecules of gases in 1811?

9   Which Greek astronomer claimed that the Earth was a cylinder at the centre of the Universe?

10 What was the name of the Greek and Roman god of medicine?

Answers on page 183

1   Who commanded the *Revenge* against the Spanish fleet in 1591, and was immortalized in a poem by Tennyson?

2   What tragedy brought Charles Lindbergh back into the public eye, five years after his famous flight?

3   Who was the mayor of West Berlin and chancellor of West Germany who had been an anti-Nazi resistance fighter in Norway?

4   Which English poet died in Greece in 1824 and became a Greek national hero?

5   Which US soldier plotted to betray West Point to the British in 1780?

6   Which Irish revolutionary leader declared that 'Bloodshed is a cleansing and sanctifying thing'?

7   In 1429, which city's siege was raised by troops led by Joan of Arc?

8   Which French hero was killed with his friend Oliver at Roncesvalles in 778?

9   Who was the tyrannical Austrian ruler killed by William Tell after he had shot the apple from his son's head?

10 Which French revolutionary leader was stabbed by Charlotte Corday?

Answers on page 183

1   What kind of bank issues currency for a nation's government?

2   What is the interest rate charged by commercial banks to their best customers?

3   Of which singer did his manager say 'When I first knew him, he had a million dollars' worth of talent: now he has a million dollars'?

4   What is the meaning of *perestroika*, the name of the programme of economic reforms introduced by Mikhail Gorbachev?

5   In which city did the Rothschild banking family first set up in business?

6   What colour are the flowers of the pennyroyal plant?

7   Which city has the oldest stock exchange?

8   Whose law states that 'bad money tends to drive out good money from circulation'?

9   Who was the British chancellor of the Exchequer who died in 1970 shortly after taking office?

10   Whose last words were to ask about the receipts at Madison Square Garden?

Answers on page 183

1   What do potatoes and dahlias produce for vegetative reproduction?

2   What is the fruit of the blackthorn tree called?

3   What are the powdered leaves of *Nicotiana* used for?

4   Which country does the Venus flytrap come from?

5   What is the name of the red palm fruit commonly chewed in Malaysia and Papua New Guinea?

6   What useful drug is extracted from the bark of the cinchona tree?

7   What kind of insect does a plant known as a myrmecophyte live with?

8   What herb, known as *Petroselinum crispum*, is a member of the carrot family?

9   What essential nutrient is present in brown rice but not in white?

10 What fruit grows on a *Cydonia oblonga* tree?

Answers on page 183

Opera

1   How did Covent Garden get its name?

2   Who pioneered the Romantic style in opera?

3   Whose operas include *Cunning Little Vixen* of 1924?

4   Who failed to complete his operas *Khovanshchina* and *Sorochintsy Fair*?

5   By what name is Shostakovich's *Lady Macbeth of Mezensk* better known?

6   What is Alessandro Moreschi, who died in Rome in 1922, famous for being?

7   Who wrote the opera *Dido and Aeneas* in 1689?

8   Who urged his librettists to 'produce a libretto that would move the world'?

9   Which style of opera did Pergolesi help to develop in Italy?

10 Which powerful backer did Gluck have in a battle between the French and Italian styles of opera in Paris in the late 1770s?

Answers on page 184

1   What small bird, of the order Passeriformes, has a
    curved bill and uplifted tail?

2   Which company made the first jet plane?

3   Which millionaire industrialist turned producer made
    the film *Hell's Angels* about World War I aviators?

4   'Open plenum' and 'peripheral jet' are types of what?

5   What is the function of a fly's hind wings?

6   Which mythological aviator plunged to his death when
    the wax in his feathers melted?

7   Who built the first successful helicopter?

8   Which aviation company developed the Harrier jump
    jet in 1966?

9   How does an autogiro differ from a helicopter?

10 Which World War II flying ace opened his first Home
    for the Incurably Sick in 1948?

Answers on page 184

1   In Greek mythology, which sorceress, the daughter of the king of Colchis, fell in love with Jason?

2   Which queen came to the throne of Denmark in 1972?

3   Which county of Ireland was once known as Queen's County?

4   What happened to queen Caroline at the coronation of her husband George IV?

5   Which French queen was the mother of the kings Francis II, Charles IX, and Henry III?

6   Which empress' claim was challenged in the War of the Austrian Succession?

7   After which queen is the Norwegian sector of Antarctica named?

8   Which Pacific country was ruled by Queen Salote until her death in 1965?

9   Which queen ruled Egypt with kings Thothmes I, II, and III?

10 Who wrote the children's story 'The Princess and the Goblin' in 1872?

Answers on page 184

1　　What is ling also known as?

2　　What is marsh gas?

3　　What is myopia commonly known as?

4　　What is thiamine usually called?

5　　What is nacre?

6　　What is a *Quercus robur*?

7　　What is the common name for Polaris?

8　　What is *Psilocybe* commonly called?

9　　What fruit is a *Ribes nigrum*?

10　　What kind of bird is a *Corvus corax*?

Answers on page 184

1   On which motor racing circuit was Ayrton Senna killed in 1994?

2   Who broke his own world 1500 metres record in 1995?

3   What kind of craft was *Hoverspeed Great Britain*, which crossed the Atlantic in less than four days in 1990?

4   Who directed the 1991 film *The Silence of the Lambs*?

5   By what name was the Football League Cup known from 1991?

6   Who was the British architect, designer of the Staatsgalerie in Stuttgart, who died in 1992?

7   In which country did President Phoumsavan succeed President Phomvihane in 1992?

8   Which composer's opera *Gawain* was first produced in 1991?

9   What was unique about the ornithopter demonstrated in the USA in 1992?

10 Which novelist published *Time's Arrow* in 1991 and *The Information* in 1995?

Answers on page 185

1   In which war is the novel *The Red Badge of Courage* set?

2   Which American general wrote that 'In war, nothing is impossible, provided you use audacity'?

3   Which great writer was wounded in the Battle of Lepanto?

4   Who defeated the British army at Majuba?

5   Who gave the name the Wars of the Roses to the struggles between the houses of Lancaster and York?

6   Where did General Cornwallis surrender, bringing to an end the American War of Independence?

7   With whom did the Japanese fight a war in 1904–05?

8   Which English king was victorious at the Battle of Crecy?

9   General Sherman in 1880 said 'There is many a boy here today who looks on war as all glory, but boys, it is all . . .' what?

10   Which military device was invented by Ernest Swinton?

Answers on page 185

1   Where are T lymphocytes produced?

2   What part of the blood do haemophiliacs lack?

3   What element makes up 65% of the human body by weight?

4   Where is oestrogen produced?

5   What is the common name for the pinna?

6   How many bones are there in the adult human?

7   Where are the metatarsals?

8   What disease is caused by lack of dopamine?

9   Where is the cochlea?

10 What is the brown pigment that gives colour to the skin, eyes, and hair?

Answers on page 185

1   To what age was the school-leaving age raised by the 1918 Education Act?

2   Who wrote *The Young Person's Guide to the Orchestra*?

3   Who became king of Egypt at the age of about 11 in the 14th century BC?

4   Who was the Italian educationalist who introduced an informal system of teaching using instructive play?

5   What was the name of the magic land created by C S Lewis in such books as *The Lion, the Witch and the Wardrobe*?

6   During whose reign were the princes murdered in the Tower?

7   Who went in search of the Woozle?

8   In which country were 12 boy pages among 22 people put to death in the 1880s by King Mwanga for refusing to renounce Christianity?

9   Which playwright called his autobiography *Borstal Boy*?

10   Which American lawyer said 'When I was a boy, I was told that anybody could become president; I'm beginning to believe it'?

Answers on page 185

1   What coloured expression is used to describe someone who wields power behind the scenes?

2   Which painter's name refers to his father's occupation as a dyer?

3   What kind of novels did Zane Grey write?

4   Whose novel *The Color Purple* won a Pulitzer prize and was filmed by Steven Spielberg?

5   What was the former name of the British Green Party?

6   What country's national emblem is the golden flower of the wattle?

7   What colour are the rocks from which the ancient city of Petra is carved?

8   What pigment gives colour to tomatoes and oranges?

9   Which country's main political parties are the Colorado (the Reds) and the Blanco (the Whites)?

10   Towards the end of its life, a star like our Sun swells up into a giant of which colour?

Answers on page 185

1   What did Karl Jansky discover about the Milky Way?

2   Who discovered the first law of thermodynamics?

3   Who invented Teflon?

4   Which Irish physicist pioneered a temperature scale?

5   Who put forward the wave theory of light?

6   Who invented the process for making ammonia?

7   Which biochemist discovered the citric acid cycle?

8   Who won the Nobel Prize for Medicine in 1960 for work on tissue transplants?

9   Who discovered jumping genes in 1983?

10   What subject was Joseph Niepce the first to photograph in 1826?

Answers on page 185

1   Which dissident Russian writer was expelled from the USSR in 1974 for his exposé of the Soviet labour camp system?

2   In which US state did Ferdinand and Imelda Marcos settle after their expulsion from the Philippines in 1986?

3   In which country did Lord Byron settle after leaving England in 1816?

4   In which year was Ayatollah Khomeini exiled from Iran before his return in 1979?

5   Which Jewish scientist emigrated to the USA in 1933 after the Nazis deprived him of his post as Director of the Kaiser Wilhelm Institute in Berlin?

6   Which leading 19th-century Italian nationalist spent much of his life in exile in England?

7   Which English Hollywood actor left the USA for Switzerland in 1952 after being accused of communist sympathies during the McCarthy witch-hunt era?

8   Which 19th-century Scottish writer, renowned for his adventure stories, spent the last years of his life at Vailima in Samoa?

9   Which influential American rock guitarist moved to England in 1966 and soon achieved the success that had eluded him in his home country?

10 The painting, *A Bigger Splash*, is typical of the Californian style of which expatriate English artist?

Answers on page 186

1   What did astronomer Giuseppe Piazzi discover in
        1801?

2   Who patented the jet engine in 1930?

3   What light-emitting device did Maiman develop in
        1963?

4   In which country was the first monorail built?

5   Who invented the sextant?

6   What particles did J J Thomson discover in 1897?

7   Who discovered the moons of Jupiter?

8   Which ancient city was discovered by Hiram Bingham
        in 1911?

9   Who discovered electromagnetic induction in 1831?

10   What did Anton van Leeuwenhoek invent in 1677?

Answers on page 186

1   What is the name of the 14 crosses that mark Christ's journey to the Crucifixion?

2   What were the characters from the earliest Germanic alphabet, often scratched on wood or stone?

3   What symbol appears in the middle of the flag of Rwanda?

4   How do the howling dervishes show the miraculous feats possible for those who trust in Allah?

5   Who directed the 1932 film epic *The Sign of the Cross*?

6   Who was acknowledged as the leader of the Symbolist poets?

7   What colour are the distinctive stripes of the Colorado beetle?

8   What is the badge of the Special Air Service?

9   In which branch of fortune-telling would you encounter the major and minor arcana?

10   In the French Revolution, what was the distinguishing sign of the working classes, as opposed to the aristocrats and the bourgeoisie?

Answers on page 186

1   In which year was Jupiter's Great Red Spot first observed?

2   How many moons has Neptune?

3   What is the largest planetary satellite of Jupiter called?

4   Which planet takes 1.88 years to orbit the Sun?

5   Which planet has an atmosphere made mostly of methane?

6   What emission was used to first identify quasars?

7   Which month did Neil Armstrong first walk on the Moon?

8   Which giant red star is also known as Alpha Orionus?

9   What are the two main constituents of Jupiter?

10   What kind of galaxy is the Milky Way?

Answers on page 186

ANSWERS

Answers to the questions in this book are followed by an entry in brackets. This shows where you can look up the answer in *The Hutchinson Encyclopedia* and find further information.

1   General Knowledge

1   Japan (tea)
2   Static electricity (static electricity)
3   He wanted to marry a divorcee (abdication crisis)
4   On the outside (skin)
5   The vernal and autumnal equinoxes (equinox)
6   Peter Rabbit (Potter)
7   Canterbury (*Canterbury Tales, The*)
8   German (Becker)
9   Ballet (Nijinsky)
10 Mathematics (Carroll)

2   Pioneers and Firsts

1   Fly in space (Gagarin)
2   Roald Amundsen (Amundsen)
3   Comic strip (comic strip)
4   Marco Polo (Polo)
5   Thomas Edison (Edison)
6   Francis Drake (Drake)
7   Orville and Wilbur (Wright)
8   Swimming the English Channel (Channel swimming)
9   Margaret Thatcher (Thatcher)
10 Al Jolson (Jolson)

3   Colours

1   Alcohol (breathalyzer)
2   Purple (Prince)
3   Bright blue (flax)
4   Iris (eye)
5   Yellow (sulphur)
6   White (United States of America – panel)
7   Blue (woad)
8   Joseph (Lloyd Webber)
9   Seven (mnemonic)
10 Red Sea (Exodus)

4   First Names

1   William (Pitt, *the Elder*; Pitt, *the Younger*)
2   Boutros (Boutros-Ghali)
3   Armstrong (Armstrong)
4   Emma (Austen)
5   Moore (Moore)
6   Percy (Percy; Shelley)
7   Johann (Bach; Strauss)
8   Kennedy (Kennedy)
9   Groucho (Marx Brothers)
10 Eric (Cantona; Eric the Red)

5   What's Up Doc?

1   The skin goes yellow (jaundice)
2   Heart attack (heart attack)
3   In the eye (eye)
4   Dreaming (dream; sleep)
5   The nerves, brain, and spinal cord (neurology)
6   2 kg (liver)
7   2 (heart)
8   Vitamin C (scurvy)
9   In vitro fertilization (in vitro fertilization)
10 Bubonic plague (Black Death)

6   1960s

1   Dwight Eisenhower (Eisenhower)
2   The Rolling Stones (Rolling Stones, the)
3   Rod Laver (Laver)
4   Synthesizer (synthesizer)
5   Gary Sobers (Sobers)
6   *Catch-22* (Heller)
7   Cuba (Cuban missile crisis)
8   Bobby Moore (Moore, Bobby)
9   Canada (Trudeau)
10 Berlin (Berlin Wall)

7   Kings and Princes

1 Henry VII (Henry VII)
2 Russia (Romanov dynasty)
3 Wilhelm II (Wilhelm II)
4 Guillotined (Louis XVI)
5 Denmark (*Hamlet*)
6 Jamaica (Jamaica; Kingston)
7 Lawn tennis (King, Billie Jean)
8 Six (George)
9 Belgium (Leopold III)
10 William and Henry (or Harry) (Charles)

8   Mountains

1 Noah (Ararat)
2 Mount Sinai (Sinai, Mount)
3 Italy (Apennines)
4 Montréal (Montréal)
5 Maiden (Jungfrau)
6 K2 (K2)
7 Rocky Mountains (Rocky Mountains)
8 St Moritz (St Moritz)
9 Balkans (Balkans)
10 1950s (Everest, Mount; mountaineering)

9   Science Selection

1 Copper and zinc (brass)
2 Elements (periodic table of the elements)
3 Glass (optical fibre)
4 Five (starfish)
5 A peat bog (Lindow Man)
6 Burning for fuel (lignite)
7 Tungsten (light bulb)
8 Charles Lindbergh (Lindbergh)
9 Copper (copper; malachite)
10 Acidity (pH)

10   Names and Titles

1 Academy Award (Academy Award)
2 Rita Hayworth (Hayworth)
3 My Struggle (*Mein Kampf*)
4 *Wuthering Heights* (Brontë)
5 Solidarity (Solidarity)
6 Gang of Four (Gang of Four)
7 Chequers (Chequers)
8 Maundy Thursday (Maundy Thursday)
9 The Supremes (Supremes, the)
10 The Great (Catherine II, Frederick II, Peter I)

11   Planet Earth

1 Radon (radon)
2 Aluminium (aluminium)
3 Ozone (ozone)
4 In lava flows (pumice)
5 Glaciers (glaciers)
6 Nitrogen (nitrogen cycle)
7 The Earth's shadow (eclipse)
8 5,000 tonnes (sewage disposal)
9 Hot rocks (geothermal energy)
10 They ate fish polluted with mercury (mercury)

12   1970s

1 Chess (Fischer, Bobby)
2 *Saturday Night Fever* (dance: chronology – panel)
3 Oil (Organization of Petroleum-Exporting Countries)
4 Spain (Spain)
5 *Evita* (Lloyd Webber)
6 Duke of Windsor (Edward VIII)
7 Spiro Agnew (Agnew)
8 A stack of bricks (Andre)
9 Ho Chi Minh City (Ho Chi Minh City)
10 Anthony Blunt (Blunt, Anthony)

13 General Knowledge

1 Cuba (Cuba)
2 Velcro (Velcro)
3 New Amsterdam (New York)
4 Ten (basketball)
5 Beachy Head (Beachy Head)
6 Fish (hake)
7 Mobiles (Calder)
8 Moses (Moses)
9 Morrissey (Morrissey)
10 Derby (Derby)

14 Oceans, Seas, and Lakes

1 Moon's gravity (tide – caption)
2 Mediterranean Sea (Beirut; Lebanon – map)
3 Ionian Sea (Corfu)
4 Turner (Turner)
5 Whale shark (shark)
6 English Channel (Blériot)
7 Neptune (Neptune)
8 The Pharos (lighthouse) at Alexandria (Seven Wonders of the World)
9 Denmark (Denmark)
10 On top of its head (whale)

15 Digging for Answers

1 Ethiopia (human species, origins of)
2 A Saxon ship (Sutton Hoo)
3 Dinosaurs (dinosaur)
4 In the sea (trilobite)
5 A terracotta army (Shi Huangdi)
6 Pembrokeshire, Wales (Stonehenge)
7 It was discovered to be fake (Turin shroud)
8 Four (pyramid)
9 A woolly mammoth (mammoth)
10 Giganotosaurus (dinosaur)

16 Colours in Nature

1 Black (anthracite)
2 Red or pink (garnet)
3 Grey (kangaroo)
4 Yellow (tansy)
5 Red (colour; electromagnetic waves)
6 Black on top, white underneath (killer whale)
7 Yellow (topaz)
8 White (shepherd's purse)
9 Silver (mercury)
10 Red (woodpecker)

17 Bon Appétit

1 Oysters (Whitstable)
2 Watermelon (watermelon)
3 Reims (Reims)
4 Garlic (garlic – picture)
5 Caviar (caviar)
6 Caffeine (caffeine)
7 Ostrich (ostrich – caption)
8 Turkey (turkey)
9 Switzerland (cheese)
10 Peach (peach)

18 Writers and Books

1 Arthur (Tennyson)
2 William Wordsworth
   (Wordsworth – quote)
3 *The Satanic Verses* (Rushdie)
4 Rudyard Kipling (Kipling)
5 He invented printing with
   moveable type (Gutenberg)
6 Calligraphy (calligraphy)
7 Scrolls (book)
8 Red (Mao Zedong – caption)
9 C S Lewis
10 Winston Churchill (Churchill)

19 Built World

1 Salisbury (Stonehenge)
2 San Francisco (San Francisco)
3 Medina (Medina – picture)
4 The Bastille (Bastille)
5 Athens (acropolis; Parthenon)
6 St Paul's (St Paul's Cathedral;
   Wren)
7 Switzerland and Italy (Simplon)
8 China (Grand Canal)
9 Arc de Triomphe (Arc de
   Triomphe)
10 Carnegie (Carnegie)

20 Time

1 Second (time)
2 Five (Islam)
3 Marcel Proust (Proust)
4 Dickens (Dickens)
5 *A Brief History of Time*
   (Hawking)
6 Carbon (carbon; radiocarbon
   dating)
7 Six (time)
8 1984 (Orwell)
9 Bob Dylan (Dylan)
10 180° (International Date Line)

21 Actors

1 Roger Moore (Moore)
2 *Rocky* (Stallone)
3 The actors' trade union (Equity)
4 'Great Stone Face' (Keaton)
5 She married Prince Rainier of
   Monaco (Kelly, Grace)
6 Laurence Olivier (Olivier)
7 Michael Caine (Caine)
8 *Big* (Hanks)
9 Stan and Oliver (Laurel and
   Hardy)
10 Richard Attenborough
   (Attenborough, Richard)

22 Animal Crackers

1 Africa (aardvark)
2 Flamingoes (flamingo)
3 A fish (grayling)
4 Hippopotamus (hippopotamus)
5 Fireflies (firefly)
6 Hedgehog (hedgehog)
7 Albatross (albatross)
8 Plants (kangaroo)
9 Bees (bee)
10 Kiwi (kiwi)

23 Discovery and Invention

1 Vacuum cleaner (vacuum
   cleaner)
2 Petroleum (plastic)
3 1866 (torpedo)
4 The mercury thermometer
   (thermometer)
5 Vacuum flask (vacuum flask)
6 Cooking (Quorn)
7 George Eastman (Eastman)
8 Helicopter (helicopter)
9 Sound recording (magnetic tape)
10 Bakelite (Bakelite)

24   Pairs

1 Ginger Rogers (Rogers; Astaire)
2 Josephine (Napoleon; Josephine)
3 Italy (Punch)
4 Trinidad (Trinidad and Tobago)
5 Gilbert and Sullivan (Gilbert, W S; Sullivan, Arthur)
6 Charles Dickens (Dickens)
7 Christopher Dean (Torvill and Dean)
8 Rib (Adam)
9 Bertie Wooster (Wodehouse)
10 Kensington (Kensington and Chelsea)

25   General Knowledge

1 Furniture design (Chippendale)
2 Butterfly (swimming)
3 Newmarket (Newmarket)
4 Jimmy Carter (Carter; Reagan)
5 Robert Redford (Redford)
6 Ass (donkey; ass)
7 Handel (Handel)
8 Czech (Lendl)
9 Philately (philately)
10 Musical instrument (spinet)

26   Islands

1 Greenland (Greenland)
2 Captain Cook (Cook, James; Hawaii)
3 Capri (Capri)
4 Japan (Japan)
5 Venice (Venice)
6 New York Harbor (Ellis Island)
7 Easter Island (Easter Island)
8 Manhattan (Manhattan)
9 Treasure Island (Stevenson)
10 Jamaica (Marley)

27   1980s

1 Ethiopia (Geldof)
2 Bob Hawke (Hawke)
3 Star Wars (Strategic Defense Initiative)
4 *Spycatcher* (Wright, Peter)
5 Sarah Ferguson (Andrew)
6 Helmut Schmidt (Germany – panel; Schmidt)
7 Michael Douglas (Academy Awards – panel)
8 Dire Straits (Dire Straits)
9 Seoul (Korea, South – panel)
10 *Crocodile Dundee* (Hogan)

28   Family Affairs

1 Music (Scarlatti)
2 Kenneth Branagh and Emma Thompson (Branagh; Thompson, Emma)
3 Robert (Kennedy)
4 Caesar (Caesar)
5 Flying (Montgolfier)
6 Windsor (Windsor, House of)
7 Fonda (Fonda, Henry; Fonda, Jane)
8 Haiti (Duvalier; Haiti)
9 Fairy tales (Grimm brothers)
10 Michael Redgrave (Redgrave)

29   Name the Year

1 1918 (World War I)
2 55 BC (Caesar)
3 1666 (London)
4 Model T Ford (Ford)
5 1961 (Gagarin)
6 1990 (Thatcher)
7 1987 (Jackson, Michael)
8 1981 (Charles; Diana)
9 1066 (Hastings, Battle of)
10 1994 (World Cup)

30   Bits and Bytes

1 Bit (bit)
2 Wide area network (wide area network)
3 Viruses (virus)
4 Disc Operating System (DOS)
5 IBM (IBM)
6 Through the telephone line (modem)
7 Beginners All-purpose Symbolic Instruction Code (BASIC)
8 Supercomputer (supercomputer)
9 Printer (printer)
10 Hard disk (output device)

31   Technology and Communication

1 Ruby (laser; ruby)
2 Alexander Graham Bell (Bell)
3 Ammonia (Haber process)
4 Semaphore (semaphore)
5 Television (television)
6 Sony (Sony)
7 Compact Disc Read Only Memory (CD-ROM)
8 In a weaving loom (loom)
9 Quartz (piezoelectric effect)
10 Printing (printing; typography)

32   Rivers

1 Pest (Budapest)
2 To stop high tides flooding London (Thames; Thames barrier)
3 John Wayne (Wayne, John)
4 USA and Canada (Niagara Falls)
5 Khartoum (Nile; Khartoum)
6 Louisiana (Louisiana)
7 Amazon (Amazon)
8 Rubicon (Rubicon)
9 Thames (Henley Royal Regatta)
10 Florence (Florence)

33   Early Scientists

1 Friction (physics – chronology)
2 Neptune (Leverrier)
3 Greek (Pythagoras)
4 In the solar spectrum (physics – chronology)
5 Fire (Heraclitus)
6 Volta (Volta)
7 Leonardo da Vinci (Leonardo da Vinci)
8 Submarine (sea transport – chronology)
9 Sewing machine (Singer)
10 That it has a magnetic field, north to south (Gilbert, William)

34   Heroes and Villains

1 Sherlock Holmes (Doyle; Holmes, Sherlock)
2 King Arthur (Tintagel)
3 007 (Fleming, Ian)
4 Spartacus (Spartacus)
5 Heracles (Heracles)
6 Abolition of slavery (Brown)
7 Laurence Oates (Oates)
8 Samson (Samson)
9 Home-made armour (Kelly, Ned)
10 Indiana Jones (Spielberg)

35   Money

1   Cent (dollar)
2   Monaco (Monaco – panel)
3   Tax haven (tax haven)
4   Clint Eastwood (Eastwood)
5   Barings (Barings)
6   Monetarism (monetarism)
7   Robert Maxwell (Maxwell, Robert)
8   Value added tax (taxation)
9   30 pieces of silver (Judas Iscariot)
10   Fort Knox (Fort Knox)

36   Plant Posers

1   Truffles (truffle)
2   Sugar (sugar)
3   Yew (yew)
4   Barley (whisky)
5   Cashew nut (cashew)
6   Soya beans (soya bean)
7   Giant redwood (sequoia)
8   Oak (oak)
9   Shamrock (shamrock)
10   The bark of a tree (cork)

37   Babies' Names

1   Tadpole (frog)
2   A mule (mule)
3   In the earth (earwig)
4   Hares (hare)
5   A cub (lion)
6   Sea horse (sea horse)
7   Pod (whale)
8   Elver (eel)
9   Salmon (salmon)
10   In their mother's pouch (koala)

38   General Knowledge

1   Heat (kelvin)
2   Swimming (Spitz)
3   William Shakespeare (Hathaway)
4   Cello (Rostropovich)
5   Basketball (basketball)
6   Chickens (poultry)
7   Führer (Hitler)
8   Textiles (Arkwright)
9   Oklahoma City (Oklahoma)
10   Smoke signals (conclave)

39   Queens and Princesses

1   Elizabeth I (Elizabeth I)
2   *Alice's Adventures in Wonderland* (*Alice's Adventures in Wonderland*)
3   Helen (Helen)
4   Princess Royal (Anne)
5   Egypt (Nefertiti)
6   Eugenie (Andrew)
7   *Macbeth* (*Macbeth*)
8   David (David)
9   Victoria (Victoria)
10   Bloody Mary (Mary I)

40   Fight, Flight, or Fright

1   White (judo)
2   The Alamo (Alamo, the; Crockett)
3   *Frankenstein* (*Frankenstein*; Shelley, Mary)
4   Tanks (Somme, Battle of the; tank)
5   Christopher Lee (Lee, Christopher)
6   Roadrunner (roadrunner)
7   Usher (Poe)
8   Duelling (duel)
9   Muhammad Ali (Ali)
10   Three minutes (boxing)

1   Maastricht (Maastricht Treaty)
2   Al Gore (Gore)
3   Michael Heseltine (Heseltine)
4   Oasis (Oasis)
5   Tom Hanks (Hanks)
6   Lebanon (Lebanon; Waite)
7   Archbishop of Canterbury
    (Canterbury, archbishop of)
8   Rwanda (Rwanda)
9   Quentin Tarantino (Tarantino)
10   Hubble (Hubble Space
    Telescope)

42   Wars and Battles

1   Gettysburg (Gettysburg)
2   Marathon (marathon; Marathon,
    Battle of)
3   Normans (Hereward)
4   East Sussex (Hastings, Battle of)
5   Napoleonic War (*War and
    Peace*)
6   Armageddon (Armageddon)
7   Spain (Trafalgar, Battle of)
8   Poland (World War II –
    chronology)
9   Machine gun (machine gun)
10   Spanish Civil War (Hemingway)

43   Human Body

1   In the brain (pituitary gland)
2   Water (human body)
3   Achilles tendon (Achilles tendon)
4   Stomach (stomach)
5   Cranium (cranium)
6   Keratin (nails)
7   Food (alimentary canal)
8   40 (pregnancy)
9   Sense of smell (nose)
10   24 (spine)

44   Kids' Stuff

1   Romans (Astérix the Gaul)
2   Disneyland (Disney)
3   Bow Bells (Bow Bells)
4   Mozart (Mozart)
5   Jodie Foster (Foster)
6   Fauntleroy (Burnett)
7   Kermit the Frog (Henson)
8   Youth Hostels Association
    (Youth Hostels Association)
9   *Cider with Rosie* (Lee, Laurie)
10   Dublin (U2 – caption)

45   Colours

1   Yellow (Baum – quote)
2   Green (billiards)
3   White (mistletoe)
4   Golf (golf)
5   White (phagocyte)
6   Yellow (Beatles, the)
7   Black (judo)
8   Green (mallard)
9   Red (ruby)
10   Blue (snooker)

46   Modern Scientists

1   Humphrey Davy (Davy)
2   Joy Adamson (Adamson, Joy)
3   Wave mechanics (Schrödinger)
4   Messenger RNA (RNA)
5   Vitamin C (vitamin)
6   Charles Darwin (Darwin, Charles)
7   Scottish (Bell)
8   Canals (Brindley)
9   Isambard Kingdom Brunel
    (Brunel)
10   Louis Pasteur (biology –
    chronology)

47   Trains, Planes, and Automobiles

1 1994 (Channel Tunnel)
2 Wood (bicycle)
3 Hovercraft (hovercraft)
4 Aircraft carriers (aircraft carrier)
5 Black box (black box)
6 London (railways – chronology)
7 By oars and sails (ship)
8 Helium (airship)
9 It was the first ship made of iron (ship)
10 France (railways)

48 Marriages and Divorces

1 Italy (Browning)
2 Mozart (Mozart)
3 Twice (Simpson, Wallis)
4 Sylvia Plath (Hughes, Ted)
5 Catherine of Aragon and Anne of Cleves (Henry VIII)
6 Douglas Fairbanks Sr (Fairbanks; Pickford)
7 Marilyn Monroe (Monroe, Marilyn)
8 Jan van Eyck (Eyck, Jan van)
9 Dustin Hoffman and Meryl Streep (Hoffman; Streep)
10 Mormon (Mormon)

49   Marks and Signs

1 Divide (mathematical symbols – panel)
2 Red (Roses, Wars of the)
3 500 (Roman numerals)
4 Legs (greenshank)
5 Libra (Libra)
6 Bar code (bar code)
7 He ordered the sea to retreat (Canute)
8 Hallmark (hallmark)
9 Symptoms (symptom)
10 Red (litmus)

50   Space: the Final Frontier

1 The Moon (Moon)
2 1969 (Armstrong, Neil)
3 The Milky Way (Milky Way)
4 Einstein (space-time)
5 Pluto (planets – panel)
6 USSR (satellite)
7 A black hole (black hole)
8 *Voyager I* (Saturn – picture)
9 Einstein (Hawking, Stephen)
10 Galileo (Galileo)

51   General Knowledge

1 Impossible (triangle)
2 Seville (orange)
3 Cambodia (Khmer)
4 Robert Dole (Dole)
5 Ukraine (Belarus; Ukraine)
6 Tony Blair (Blair – quote)
7 A fungus (*Candida albicans*)
8 Cole Porter (Porter, Cole)
9 Tax evasion (Capone)
10 Jane Austen (Austen)

52   Pioneers and Firsts

1   South Africa (Great Trek)
2   Rocketry (von Braun; rocket)
3   Penny post (Hill, Rowland)
4   Henry Wood (Wood)
5   Red Cross (Red Cross, the; Dunant)
6   Northwest Passage (Northwest Passage; Baffin; Franklin, John; Frobisher)
7   Television (Cable News Network)
8   Pop art (Pop art)
9   Jules Verne (Verne)
10   A saint (Cabrini)

53   Colours

1   The five continents (Olympic Games)
2   Red (red shift)
3   Green (crab)
4   Scarlet (Doyle, Arthur Conan)
5   Grey (wolf)
6   Red, white, and blue (Netherlands – panel)
7   White (condor)
8   Red Crescent (Red Cross, the)
9   Brown (Brownshirts)
10   Libya (Libya – panel)

54   First Names

1   Truman (Capote; Truman)
2   Lyndon (Johnson)
3   Bonnie and Clyde (Bonnie and Clyde)
4   Isambard (Brunel)
5   Randolph (Churchill)
6   Django (Reinhardt, Django)
7   Clerihew (clerihew)
8   Edmund (Edmund II Ironside; Hillary)
9   James (James, Jesse)
10   Jacob (Esau; Jacob)

55   What's Up Doc?

1   AIDS (zidovudine)
2   Adrenal glands (Addison's disease; adrenal gland)
3   Down's syndrome (Down's syndrome)
4   None (placebo)
5   Aspirin (aspirin)
6   Teeth and gums (periodontal disease)
7   Eyes (glaucoma)
8   Snails (bilharzia)
9   Liver (hepatitis)
10   Skin (impetigo)

56   1960s

1   Greece (Greece)
2   Sri Lanka or Ceylon (Bandaranaike)
3   *2001: A Space Odyssey* (Kubrick)
4   Southern Rhodesia (Zimbabwe)
5   The Cultural Revolution (Cultural Revolution)
6   For refusing to be drafted into the army (Ali)
7   *Civilization* (Clark, Kenneth)
8   Khrushchev (Union of Soviet Socialist Republics)
9   Phil Spector (Spector)
10   Drowning (Australia)

57   Kings and Princes

1 Edward V (Edward V)
2 8th (Charlemagne)
3 Constantine II (Constantine II; Greece)
4 Spain (Spain)
5 Stephen King (King, Stephen)
6 Canada (Canada; Prince Edward Island)
7 Liechtenstein (Liechtenstein)
8 Grimaldi (Monaco)
9 Edward VI (Edward VI; Henry VIII)
10 Judaea (Herod the Great)

58   Mountains

1 Bhutan (Bhutan)
2 In a desert (desert)
3 Matterhorn (Matterhorn; mountaineering; Whymper)
4 Observatories (Mount Palomar; Mount Wilson)
5 Mount St Helens (St Helens, Mount)
6 New Zealand (New Zealand – panel)
7 Atlas Mountains (Atlas Mountains)
8 Austria and Italy (Brenner Pass)
9 Caucasus (Caucasus; Elbruz)
10 Africa (Drakensberg)

59   Science Selection

1 Opium (opium)
2 Hg (periodic table of the elements)
3 In the intestines (peristalsis)
4 Fox (fox)
5 Electrical charge (capacitor)
6 Goat (Capricornus)
7 A baboon (mandrill)
8 A plant (Solomon's seal)
9 Signalling in Morse code (heliography)
10 Cep (fungus)

60   Names and Titles

1 The Leader (Mussolini)
2 William Pitt the Elder (Pitt *the Elder*)
3 Duke of York (George VI)
4 Military Intelligence (intelligence)
5 Jack Nicklaus (Nicklaus)
6 Aircraft (HOTOL; VSTOL)
7 Salop (Salop)
8 *General Belgrano* (*General Belgrano*)
9 Dutch auction (Dutch auction)
10 Blood and Guts (Patton)

1. Natural Environment Research Council (Natural Environment Research Council)
2. Peat (fossil fuel; peat)
3. Water (hydrology)
4. Exxon Corporation, or Esso (Exxon Corporation)
5. Wind speed (Beaufort scale)
6. 250 (Chernobyl)
7. Hydroelectric power (hydroelectric power)
8. Arctic Circle (Arctic Circle)
9. 50 (endangered species)
10. Water (aquifer)

1. Bangladesh (Bangladesh)
2. National Theatre (Lasdun)
3. *Life on Earth* (Attenborough, David)
4. Tom Stoppard (Stoppard)
5. Standard Oil (Exxon Corporation)
6. Amnesty International (Amnesty International)
7. *One Flew Over the Cuckoo's Nest* (Nicholson, Jack)
8. Valéry Giscard d'Estaing (Giscard d'Estaing)
9. Birmingham (Birmingham Six)
10. John Betjeman (Betjeman)

1. Belly (meat – diagram)
2. Battle of Jutland (Jutland, Battle of)
3. A wind (chinook)
4. Kenny Dalglish (Dalglish)
5. Denmark (Christian X)
6. Burnt down (Crystal Palace)
7. So that the finish was in front of the royal box (marathon)
8. Stirling Moss (Moss)
9. Jack Hobbs (Hobbs)
10. I (Morse code)

1. Germany, Austria, and Switzerland (Constance, Lake)
2. Giant's Causeway (Giant's Causeway)
3. Lake Superior (Great Lakes; Superior, Lake)
4. Tasman Sea (Tasman Sea)
5. Andes (Titicaca)
6. Battle of Actium (Actium, Battle of)
7. Chinese (sea transport – panel)
8. Gulf of Guinea (Ivory Coast)
9. The Sleeve (Channel, English)
10. Francis Chichester (Chichester)

65   Modern Music

1 Hoagy Carmichael (Carmichael)
2 Sitar (Shankar)
3 Bluebeat (ska)
4 Skiffle (skiffle)
5 *Night Music* (Sondheim)
6 Tuba (sousaphone)
7 Thomson (Thomson, Virgil)
8 Bessie Smith (Smith, Bessie)
9 New York (rap music)
10 'The Great Pretender' (doo-wop)

66   Number Crunching

1 One light year (light year)
2 Magnetic flux (maxwell)
3 Precious metals and gems (troy system)
4 Pressure (pascal; pressure)
5 Energy (joule)
6 Amperes (ampere)
7 Watts (watt)
8 Hertz (hertz)
9 9 (giga-; SI units – prefixes)
10 Radioactivity (becquerel)

67   Seasons

1 Igor Stravinsky (Stravinsky)
2 *Richard III* (Shakespeare; winter of discontent)
3 St John the Baptist (John the Baptist, St; midsummer)
4 three: the cold, the hot, and the rainy (monsoon; season)
5 St Petersburg (St Petersburg)
6 James Thomson (Thomson, James)
7 Botticelli (Botticelli)
8 Thomas More (Scofield)
9 USSR and Finland (Winter War)
10 Autumn crocus (autumn crocus)

68   Writers and Books

1 John Le Carré (Le Carré – caption)
2 George Bernard Shaw (Shaw)
3 *The Grapes of Wrath* (Steinbeck)
4 China (Buck)
5 At King Arthur's Court (Twain)
6 Robinson Crusoe (*Robinson Crusoe*)
7 Algeria (Camus)
8 Emile Zola (Zola)
9 Kazuo Ishiguro (Booker Prize for Fiction)
10 Detective novels (Hammett)

69   Built World

1 Wisconsin (Yerkes Observatory)
2 The Eiffel Tower (Eiffel Tower)
3 Castle (castle)
4 Kew Gardens (Chambers; Kew Gardens)
5 Apollo (Colossus of Rhodes)
6 The Crystal Palace (Crystal Palace; Great Exhibition)
7 Norman (Norman architecture; Romanesque)
8 Tate Gallery (Stirling, James)
9 White (Taj Mahal)
10 Observatory (observatory)

70   Time

1 Dancing (Novello)
2 Salvador Dali (Dali)
3 Leo (zodiac)
4 Six days (Israel)
5 Five years (five-year plan)
6 J B Priestley (Priestley, J B)
7 15 minutes (Warhol – quote)
8 Count Basie (Basie)
9 Once a week (magazine)
10 Gary Cooper (Cooper, Gary)

71 Actors

1 Lauren Bacall (Bacall; Bogart)
2 Alfred Hitchcock (Grant, Cary; Hitchcock)
3 *The Accused* (Academy Awards – panel; Foster, Jodie)
4 Frank Sinatra (Sinatra)
5 Paul Newman (Newman, Paul)
6 Charlie Chaplin (Attenborough)
7 Abraham Lincoln (Booth, John Wilkes)
8 Judy Garland (Garland)
9 Robert Redford (Redford)
10 *The Wild One* (Brando)

72 Animal Crackers

1 2 (alligator)
2 Snail (abalone)
3 A beetle (cochineal)
4 Racoon (racoon)
5 In burrows (bandicoot)
6 Water (manatee)
7 A fish (roach)
8 Scorpions (scorpion)
9 Vampire bat (vampire bat)
10 Pied wagtail (wagtail)

73 Origin of the Species

1 Chimpanzee (human species, origins of)
2 *Homo sapiens sapiens* (human species, origins of)
3 40,000 years (human species, origins of)
4 19th century (Darwin)
5 Plants (dinosaurs)
6 Richard Dawkins (Dawkins)
7 Pleistocene (Pleistocene)
8 Lamarck (Lamarckism)
9 Austrian (Mendel)
10 Mammals (mammals; evolution)

74 Pairs

1 William Abbott (Abbot and Costello)
2 Faye Dunaway (Dunaway)
3 Paul McCartney (McCartney)
4 Ravel (Ravel)
5 Genesis (Sodom and Gomorrah)
6 St Paul (Minneapolis)
7 All directed by Stan Laurel (Laurel and Hardy)
8 Paris (Nureyev)
9 Bertolt Brecht (Weill; Brecht)
10 Neptune (Neptune)

75 General Knowledge

1 Belgium (Spa)
2 Prince Charles (Charles; Diana)
3 Death Valley (Death Valley)
4 Raglan (Raglan)
5 Czech Republic (Semtex)
6 Music (Falla)
7 Henry Shrapnel (Shrapnel)
8 Crucified (Spartacus)
9 John Surtees (Surtees)
10 Bud Flanagan (Flanagan)

76 Islands

1 Honshu (Tokyo)
2 New Guinea (island – panel)
3 France (Madagascar)
4 Isle of Ely (Ely)
5 Canary Islands (Lanzarote)
6 Crete (Icarus)
7 Windward Islands (Antilles)
8 W B Yeats (Yeats)
9 Singapore (Singapore – panel)
10 Tahiti (Gauguin)

1 Oliver Stone (Academy Awards – panel)
2 Calgary (Calgary)
3 P W Botha (Botha)
4 Sebastian Coe (Coe)
5 Allan Border (Border)
6 Ted Hughes (Hughes)
7 Dudley Moore (Moore)
8 Andropov (USSR – panel)
9 Kingsley Amis (Amis, Kingsley; Booker Prize for Fiction)
10 Nigel Kennedy (Kennedy, Nigel)

78 Family Affairs

1 Alexandre Dumas (Dumas)
2 Dostoevsky (Dostoevsky)
3 Lumière (Lumière)
4 Chamberlain (Chamberlain)
5 Catherine of Aragon (Henry VIII)
6 Bourbon (Bourbon)
7 Mother's Day (Mother's Day)
8 No relation (Strauss, Johann; Strauss, Richard)
9 Grandfather and grandson (Harrison, Benjamin; Harrison, William)
10 Napoleon (Napoleon I)

79 Name the Year

1 1978 (John Paul I)
2 1942 (Alamein, El, Battles of)
3 1929 (Black Thursday)
4 1956 (Suez Crisis)
5 1968 (France; Prague Spring)
6 1945 (Roosevelt; Truman)
7 1984 (Muldoon; Mulroney)
8 1989 (Rushdie)
9 1649 (Charles I)
10 1977 (Presley)

80 Bits and Bytes

1 ESP (LISP; PASCAL; SQL)
2 Pixels (pixel)
3 Silicon (silicon chip)
4 What you see is what you get (WYSIWYG)
5 Graphical user interface (graphical user interface)
6 VDU (input device; VDU)
7 Santa Clara County (Silicon Valley)
8 Operating systems (MS-DOS; operating system; Unix)
9 Optical Character Recognition (OCR)
10 International Business Machines (IBM)

81 Technology and Communication

1 Postal service (postal service)
2 Printing (printing; typography)
3 Rubber (rubber; vulcanization)
4 Typefaces or founts (typeface)
5 Ultrasound (ultrasound scanning)
6 Unilever (Unilever)
7 Sodium carbonate (Solvay process)
8 Stainless steel (stainless steel)
9 Teflon (Teflon)
10 London and Slough (telecommunications)

82   Rivers

1 They were named after the aviator James Angel (Angel Falls)
2 Australia (Murray)
3 Rio de Janeiro (Rio de Janeiro)
4 Niger (Niger; Nigeria)
5 Clyde (Clydebank)
6 Caspian Sea (Volga)
7 Seine (Paris; Seine)
8 A tidal wave (Severn)
9 Bayou (bayou; oxbow lake)
10 Lisbon (Tagus; Lisbon)

83   Early Scientists

1 Galen (Galen)
2 Galileo (Galileo)
3 Thomas Linacre (Linacre)
4 Linnaeus (Linnaeus)
5 Tuberculosis (Koch)
6 Isaac Newton (Newton; physics – chronology)
7 Pythagoras (Pythagoras)
8 Newton (Newton)
9 Archimedes (Archimedes; physics – chronology)
10 Hippocrates (Hippocrates; biology – chronology)

84   Flight

1 Oregon (Boeing)
2 Amy Johnson (Johnson, Amy)
3 Alan Shepard (Shepard, Alan)
4 Hydrogen (airship)
5 Peter Pan (*Peter Pan*)
6 Lockheed (Lockheed)
7 *Challenger* (space shuttle)
8 Hedge sparrow (dunnock)
9 Thrush (nightingale)
10 Glider (flight – chronology)

85   Money

1 Chinese (money)
2 Green pound (green pound)
3 Blue chip (blue chip)
4 Punt (Ireland, Republic of – panel)
5 Oil (Rockefeller)
6 Croesus (Croesus)
7 Ghana (Ghana; Gold Coast)
8 Aaron (Golden Calf)
9 Kibbutz (kibbutz)
10 Giro (giro)

86   Plant Posers

1 Silk (silk)
2 An algae (seaweed)
3 Flax (flax)
4 Trefoil (trefoil)
5 Beech (beech)
6 Pea family (lupin)
7 The root (liquorice)
8 For making tea (tea)
9 Bergamot (bergamot)
10 Seakale (seakale)

87   Femmes Fatales

1 With a poisonous snake (Cleopatra)
2 Glenn Close (Close)
3 Salome (Salome)
4 Bette Davis (Davis, Bette)
5 Clytemnestra (Clytemnestra)
6 Ferrara (Borgia, Lucrezia)
7 Barbara Stanwyck (Stanwyck)
8 Journalist (Meinhof)
9 Charles II (Charles II)
10 Calypso (Calypso)

1. The speed of light, 300,000,000 metres per second (speed of light)
2. It speeds up (speed of sound)
3. Mercury (planets)
4. 27 (Moon)
5. 3 days 7 hours (sea transport)
6. 15 days (sea transport – chronology)
7. Train (railways)
8. 70–80 bpm (heart)
9. Albatross (albatross)
10. 110 kph/70 mph (cheetah)

89   Queens and Princesses

1. Netherlands (Juliana)
2. Hans Christian Andersen (Andersen)
3. Isabella I (Columbus)
4. 18th century (Catherine II)
5. John Smith (Pocahontas)
6. Glenda Jackson (Jackson, Glenda)
7. Nine days (Grey, Lady Jane)
8. Drone (bee)
9. 'America' ('God Save the Queen')
10. Shelley (Shelley)

90   Marks and Signs

1. A bundle of rods (fasces)
2. Rastafarianism (Rastafarianism)
3. Hawk (hawk)
4. Hooded white robes (Ku Klux Klan)
5. Rat (Desert Rats)
6. Whit Sunday (Whit Sunday)
7. π (mathematical symbols – panel)
8. Two keys (Peter, St)
9. Cross of Lorraine (Free French)
10. Diamonds (rattlesnake – caption)

1. Canada (Canada)
2. Governor of Hong Kong (Patten)
3. North Korea (Kim Il Sung; Kim Jong Il)
4. France (Cresson)
5. Yitzhak Rabin (Rabin)
6. Burma or Myanmar (Suu Kyi)
7. Crystal Palace (Cantona)
8. Chechnya (Russian Federation – table)
9. New York (Dinkins)
10. Somalia (Somalia – panel)

92   Wars and Battles

1. Ethiopia or Abyssinia (Ethiopia; Mussolini)
2. H G Wells (Wells)
3. A victory not worth winning (Pyrrhus)
4. Boer War (Churchill)
5. Korea (Korean War)
6. Opium (Opium Wars)
7. Iberian Peninsula (Peninsular War)
8. Vietcong (Tet Offensive)
9. A Jewish holy day (Yom Kippur War)
10. Austria and Russia (Napoleonic Wars)

93   Human Body

1 In the joints (synovial fluid)
2 The spine (scoliosis)
3 Graafian follicle (Graafian follicle)
4 During childbirth (relaxin)
5 Red blood cell (red blood cell)
6 The lymph glands (scrofula)
7 Mole (naevus)
8 On the chest (pectoral)
9 Insulin (pancreas)
10 Kidneys (kidney)

94   Kids' Stuff

1 To recapture Jerusalem (Children's Crusade)
2 A fairy dies (Barrie – quote)
3 'Peanuts' (comic strip)
4 Lewis Carroll (Carroll)
5 Babe (Ruth)
6 The American War of Independence (Rip Van Winkle)
7 Shepherd boy (David)
8 Ranger Guides (Girl Guides)
9 Rugby football (rugby)
10 Byron (Byron)

95   Opera

1 *La Bohème* (Caruso; Melba)
2 Donizetti (Donizetti)
3 Stravinksy (Auden)
4 Placido Domingo (Domingo)
5 Milan (Milan)
6 A Widow (Lehár)
7 Liszt (Wagner)
8 Venice (opera)
9 *Orpheus in the Underworld* (cancan)
10 Franco Zeffirelli (Zeffirelli)

96   Modern Scientists

1 Roads (road)
2 1941 (biochemistry – chronology)
3 Jean Foucault (Foucault, Jean)
4 Chemistry (Hodgkin, Dorothy)
5 Robert Fulton (Fulton)
6 Nuclear magnetic resonance imaging (chemistry – panel)
7 J E Thompson (archaeology – chronology)
8 Astronomy (Hoyle)
9 Darwin's theory of evolution (Huxley, Thomas)
10 Superconductivity (Josephson)

97   Trains, Planes, and Automobiles

1 Bombing London (Zeppelin)
2 C5 (Sinclair)
3 *Train à grande vitesse* (TGV)
4 1991 (Channel Tunnel)
5 They travel faster than the speed of sound (sonic boom)
6 Stockton and Darlington (railways – chronology)
7 1959 (hovercraft)
8 *Nautilus* (submarine)
9 J B Dunlop (Dunlop)
10 Sulphuric acid (battery)

1   Tarantula (tarantula)
2   Plant sap (aphid)
3   In water (caddis fly)
4   Booklouse (booklouse)
5   Ladybird (ladybird)
6   Flea (flea)
7   Jumps on to its feet from lying on its back (click beetle)
8   Paraquat (insecticide; paraquat)
9   Nothing (pupa)
10 Termites (termite)

99   Heroes and Villains

1   John Wayne (Wayne, John)
2   Iago (*Othello*)
3   Scarlett O'Hara (Leigh, Vivian)
4   Don Juan (Don Juan)
5   Claudius (*Hamlet*)
6   Quisling (Quisling)
7   Bonnie Prince Charlie (Macdonald, Flora)
8   David Copperfield (Dickens)
9   Raymond Chandler (Chandler)
10 Heinrich Himmler (Himmler; SS)

100   Space: the Final Frontier

1   Hubble Space Telescope (Hubble Space Telescope)
2   1988 (space shuttle)
3   *Luna 2* (Moon probe)
4   *Galileo* (*Galileo*)
5   Saturn (planets – panel)
6   1930 (astronomy – chronology)
7   Edwin Hubble (galaxy; Hubble)
8   Saturn (Saturn)
9   Charon (Pluto)
10 1986 (Halley's comet)

101   General Knowledge

1   Julian (Julian)
2   Jumping hare or springhare (jumping hare)
3   Aldwych (Travers)
4   White (owl)
5   New Mexico (Bainbridge, Kenneth)
6   A weedkiller (Agent Orange)
7   Leoncavallo (Leoncavallo)
8   Weaving (Arachne)
9   Otto (Otto cycle)
10 Chesney (Baker, Chet)

102   Pioneers and Firsts

1   Take a photograph (Niepce)
2   Ferdinand Magellan (Cano; Magellan)
3   Computing (Babbage; Turing)
4   Trombone (sackbut)
5   Delaware (Delaware)
6   Niger (Park)
7   HMS *Beagle* (Darwin)
8   *Voyager 2* (Voyager probes)
9   Les Paul (Paul, Les)
10 Buckminster Fuller (Fuller, Buckminster)

103   Colours

1   John Dillinger (Dillinger)
2   Brown and green (crayfish)
3   Rose (Picasso)
4   Grey (Franciscan order)
5   Red (orthochromatic)
6   *Whistler's Mother* (Whistler, James)
7   Tom Wolfe (Wolfe, Tom)
8   Red (Powell, Michael; Pressburger)
9   Rye (rye)
10 Blue and yellow (Fangio)

104   First Names

1. Jan (Eyck, Jan van; Vermeer)
2. Chauvin (chauvinism)
3. Karol (John Paul II)
4. David Wark (Griffith)
5. Allen (Allen)
6. Luke (*Hansard*)
7. Edward (Lee, Robert E)
8. Leopoldo (Galtieri)
9. Jessica (Academy Awards – panel)
10. Eleanor (Gwyn)

105   What's Up Doc?

1. Air (trachea)
2. Viral (virus)
3. Uric acid (uric acid)
4. Steroid hormones (Cushing's syndrome)
5. Epilepsy (epilepsy)
6. Skin cancer (melanoma)
7. Deep sea diving (decompression sickness)
8. In the neck (carotid artery)
9. Plasma (plasma)
10. Mining (silicosis)

106   1960s

1. Bob Beamon (Powell, Mike)
2. Los Angeles (assassination – panel)
3. Ennio Morricone (Morricone)
4. Argentina (Eichmann)
5. Jean-Paul Sartre (Sartre)
6. Portugal (Portugal; Salazar)
7. Stevie Wonder (Wonder)
8. *Unsafe at Any Speed* (car – panel)
9. Radio Atlanta (pirate radio)
10. Willy Brandt (Brandt, Willy)

107   Kings and Princes

1. Nepal (Buddha)
2. Romania (Michael)
3. Faisal (Faisal)
4. Canada (King, William)
5. Scrofula (king's evil; scrofula)
6. Eleventh (Macbeth)
7. Lesotho (Lesotho)
8. Brian Boru (Brian)
9. Prince Rupert (Rupert)
10. Charles (Charles)

108   Mountains

1. China, Pakistan, and India (Karakoram)
2. Siege style (mountaineering)
3. Mountain sickness (Andes)
4. John Huston (Huston)
5. Mexico (Sierra Madre)
6. Australia (Great Dividing Range)
7. Yosemite (Yosemite – picture)
8. Cwm (corrie)
9. Hindu Kush (Salang Highway)
10. Sri Lanka (Sri Lanka – panel)

109   Science Selection

1. Dried flower heads (pyrethrum)
2. Cirrus (cloud)
3. Fool's gold (pyrite)
4. Mercury (cinnabar)
5. Chew them (qat)
6. 1966 (petroleum – panel)
7. Glucose (cellulose)
8. Centipede (centipede)
9. Ten (crab)
10. An electron (beta particle)

110   Names and Titles

1 Emir (Kuwait)
2 Duke of Marlborough (Marlborough)
3 Cat and Mouse Act (Cat and Mouse Act)
4 The Six (*Les Six*)
5 Abbey Theatre (Abbey Theatre)
6 Missouri (Missouri)
7 Sulky (horse racing)
8 Lafayette (Lafayette)
9 Horseshoe Falls (Niagara Falls)
10 Fire engine (Newcomen)

111   Planet Earth

1 Rocks (radiometric dating)
2 Zenith (zenith)
3 Basalt (basalt)
4 Off the Pacific coast of South America (*El Niño*)
5 Aclinic line or magnetic equator (aclinic line)
6 12 (hurricane)
7 A fungus (Dutch elm disease)
8 3,660 m (ocean)
9 Coriolis effect (Coriolis effect)
10 0.00005% (atmosphere)

112   1970s

1 Juan Perón (Perón)
2 Astérix the Gaul (Astérix the Gaul)
3 E L Doctorow (Doctorow)
4 *Maurice* (Forster, E M)
5 Malcolm Williamson (Williamson, Malcolm)
6 Margaret Laurence (Laurence)
7 Lockheed (Lockheed)
9 Marlene Dietrich (Dietrich)
9 Nouvelle cuisine (nouvelle cuisine)
10 LOGO (LOGO)

113   General Knowledge

1 Australia (Christmas Island)
2 Southern Cross (Crux)
3 Purple Heart (medals and decorations; Purple Heart, Order of the)
4 Sun (Uruguay – panel)
5 Ethelred the Unready (Ethelred II)
6 Eight (crusade)
7 Hare (basset)
8 Twelve (chromatic scale)
9 Europa (Europa)
10 Java (batik)

114   Oceans, Seas, and Lakes

1 Atlantic (Cape Verde)
2 Henry (Hudson, Henry; Hudson Bay)
3 Lake Nyasa (Malawi, Lake)
4 Labrador Current (Arctic, the)
5 Sea horse (sea horse)
6 Yellow Sea (Yellow Sea)
7 Yucatan Channel (North America – map)
8 Tasmania (Great Lake)
9 Fridtjof Nansen (Nansen)
10 Coral Sea (Coral Sea)

115   What Is It?

1 Study of the function of signs and symbols (semiology)
2 Finger cymbals (cymbal)
3 Cat (serval)
4 Wound-wire coil (armature)
5 Forest zone (taiga)
6 Worm (nematode)
7 Pale-green gemstone (peridot)
8 Buddhist monk (bhikku)
9 Neutral politician (mugwump)
10 Musical instrument (spinet)

116   My Other Job

1 Arthur Conan Doyle (Doyle)
2 T S Eliot (Eliot, T S)
3 Prime minister (Paderewski)
4 Art history (Blunt, Anthony)
5 Governor-General of Canada (Buchan)
6 Writing (Conrad, Joseph)
7 John Vanbrugh (Vanbrugh)
8 Howard Hughes (Hughes, Howard)
9 George Orwell (Orwell)
10 Medicine (Grace; Guevara; Maugham)

117   Bon Appétit

1 Carrot (caraway)
2 Antonin Carême (Carême)
3 Green and yellow (Chartreuse)
4 Penicillin (cheese)
5 Pods (tamarind)
6 Third Thursday in November (Beaujolais)
7 Bats (bananas)
8 Oak (truffle)
9 Edible seaweed (seaweed)
10 Aztecs (cocoa and chocolate)

118   Writers and Books

1 Shorthand (shorthand)
2 Zinoviev letter (Zinoviev)
3 John Henry Newman (Elgar)
4 The Mambo Kings (Pulitzer Prize for Fiction – panel)
5 Confucius (Analects; Confucius)
6 Nineveh (library)
7 John Boorman (Boorman)
8 *Jane Eyre* (Rhys)
9 Ancient Egyptian (*Book of the Dead*)
10 Primo Levi (Levi)

119   Ideas and Beliefs

1 John Calvin (Calvin)
2 Edward de Bono (de Bono)
3 Constantine (Constantine the Great)
4 Taboo (taboo)
5 Joseph Heller (*Catch-22*)
6 Hinduism (suttee)
7 Spinoza (Spinoza; philosophy – panel)
8 All-enveloping black garment for women (chador; purdah)
9 Parsees (Parsee)
10 Mythical country of leisure and idleness (Cockaigne, Land of)

120   Time

1 Rosh Hashanah (Rosh Hashanah)
2 French and Indian War (Seven Years' War)
3 Friday (calendar; Freya)
4 February (Candlemas)
5 Muslim (calendar)
6 A water clock (clock)
7 Haydn (Haydn)
8 Salisbury (clock)
9 Jurassic (geological time – chart; Jurassic)
10 Alan Bennett (Bennett, Alan)

121   Actors

1   Jake LaMotta (De Niro)
2   Acrobat (Lancaster, Burt)
3   Lady Bracknell (Evans, Edith)
4   Renaissance Theatre Company (Branagh)
5   Mae West (West, Mae)
6   Henry Irving (Irving, Henry)
7   Richard Burbage (Burbage)
8   Sam Shepard (Shepard, Sam)
9   Drury Lane (Garrick)
10 Mrs Patrick Campbell (Campbell, Mrs Patrick)

122   Animal Crackers

1   House mouse (mouse)
2   Canada and Greenland (musk ox)
3   Echolocation (echolocation)
4   Beetles (beetle)
5   Shark (shark; whale)
6   A fish (manta)
7   Puffin (puffin)
8   Blackbird (blackbird)
9   Fish (characin)
10 Kodiak bear (bear)

123   Also Known As . . .

1   El Cid (Cid, El)
2   Saki (Saki)
3   Leon Trotsky (Trotsky)
4   Elvis Costello (Costello)
5   Gold (California)
6   Edinburgh (Edinburgh)
7   Boris Karloff (Karloff)
8   Kent (Kent)
9   Captain James Bigglesworth (Johns, W E)
10 Jesuits, or Society of Jesus (Jesuits)

124   Pairs

1   Verona (*Romeo and Juliet*)
2   Printing of music (Byrd; Tallis)
3   On a ship's hull (Plimsoll line)
4   A sea monster and a whirlpool (Scylla and Charybdis)
5   Cribbage (cribbage)
6   *Jules et Jim* (Moreau)
7   Oxford and Cambridge Boat Race reserve crews (Boat Race)
8   Attempting to shoot Rimbaud (Verlaine; Rimbaud)
9   Zeus and Leda (Helen)
10 Antony and Cleopatra (Barber)

125   General Knowledge

1   A group of astronomers (Celestial Police)
2   Publication of a spurious sequel by someone else (Cervantes)
3   Tuba (brass instrument)
4   Rob Roy (Rob Roy)
5   They were shoguns (shogun)
6   Siena (Siena)
7   Lizard (skink)
8   Keeping her own name after marriage (Stone, Lucy)
9   The Curragh (Curragh, the)
10 Kit Carson (Carson City)

126   Islands

1   Copenhagen (Copenhagen)
2   Volcanic eruption (Tristan da Cunha)
3   Crete (Knossos)
4   Patmos (Patmos)
5   South Africa (Robben Island)
6   Iceland (Iceland)
7   Luzon (Luzon)
8   The pancreas (pancreas)
9   Marshall Islands (Bikini)
10 St Aidan (Holy Island)

127 1980s

1 Tom Stoppard (Stoppard)
2 Mountain biking (mountain biking)
3 MacDonald's (Illinois)
4 Digital audio tape (digital audio tape)
5 Sugar Ray Leonard (Leonard)
6 United Artists (United Artists)
7 Master sergeant (Doe)
8 Ingrid Kristiansen (Kristiansen)
9 Nottingham (Torvill and Dean)
10 William Golding (Golding)

128 Family Affairs

1 William (Douglas-Home, William)
2 Forsyte (Galsworthy)
5 Edmund Spenser (Spenser)
4 Pierre-Auguste and Jean Renoir (Renoir)
5 Fairbanks (Fairbanks)
6 Aldous Huxley (Huxley, Aldous; Huxley, Thomas)
7 Grenville (Grenville, George; Grenville, William)
8 Scarlatti (Scarlatti)
9 Dukes of Norfolk (Earl Marshal; Norfolk, Miles Fitzalan- Howard)
10 Hohenzollern (Hohenzollern)

129 Name the Year

1 1943 (Bogart)
2 1841 (Harrison, William)
3 1789 (Bligh)
4 1927 (Lindbergh)
5 1779 (Cook, James)
6 1982 (Kelly)
7 1889 (Eiffel Tower)
8 1704 (Blenheim, Battle of; Marlborough)
9 1912 (Roosevelt, Theodore)
10 1979 (Iran)

130 Bits and Bytes

1 1,024 (megabyte)
2 Structured Query Language (SQL)
3 Altair 8800 (computing – panel)
4 1990 (computing – panel)
5 Artificial intelligence (PROLOG)
6 Common Business-Oriented Language (COBOL)
7 A compiler (compiler; machine code)
8 Direct Information Access Network for Europe (DIANE)
9 Musical Instrument Digital Interface (MIDI)
10 Baud (baud)

131 Technology and Communication

1 Steel (Bessemer process)
2 Shorthand (shorthand)
3 1929 (television – chronology)
4 New Haven, Connecticut (telecommunications – chronology)
5 1956 (telecommunications – chronology)
6 *Telstar* (*Telstar*)
7 625 (television)
8 Zelenchukskaya, Russia (telescope)
9 Thames (Thames Tunnel)
10 Frequency modulation (radio)

132   Rivers

1 Jumna (Ganges)
2 Turkey (meander; Menderes)
3 Uganda, Kenya, and Tanzania (Victoria, Lake)
4 Australia (Australia – map)
5 River blindness (onchocerciasis)
6 Ruhr (Ruhr)
7 Bangladesh (Bangladesh – panel)
8 Chile (Bío-Bío)
9 Nile (Valley of the Kings)
10 Thornton Wilder (Wilder, Thornton)

133   Early Scientists

1 Robert Hooke (biology – chronology; Hooke)
2 Democritus (Democritus; physics – chronology)
3 Proteins (biochemistry – chronology)
4 Plants (biology – chronology)
5 Chicken (biology – chronology)
6 Luigi Galvani (Galvani: physics – chronology)
7 Pendulum clock (Huygens; physics – chronology)
8 Avogadro (Avogadro; physics – chronology)
9 Anaximander (Anaximander)
10 Aesculapius (Aesculapius)

134   Heroes and Villains

1 Richard Grenville (Grenville, Richard)
2 His son was murdered (Lindbergh – caption)
3 Willy Brandt (Brandt)
4 Byron (Byron – caption)
5 Benedict Arnold (Arnold, Benedict)
6 Patrick Pearse (Pearse – quote)
7 Orléans (Joan of Arc, St)
8 Roland (Roland)
9 Gessler (Tell)
10 Jean-Paul Marat (Corday; Marat)

135   Money

1 Central bank (bank)
2 Prime rate (prime rate)
3 Elvis Presley (Presley – quote)
4 'Restructuring' (*perestroika*)
5 Frankfurt-am-Main (Rothschild)
6 Purple (pennyroyal)
7 Antwerp (stock exchange)
8 Gresham (Gresham)
9 Iain McLeod (McLeod)
10 Phineas T Barnum (Barnum – quote)

136   Plant Posers

1 Tubers (tuber)
2 Sloe (blackthorn)
3 Snuff (tobacco)
4 USA (Venus flytrap)
5 Betel nut (betel nut)
6 Quinine (quinine)
7 Ants (myremecophyte)
8 Parsley (parsley)
9 Vitamin B (rice)
10 Quince (quince)

1 From a convent garden once on the site (Covent Garden)
2 Weber (Weber, Carl; opera)
3 Leoš Janáček (Janáček)
4 Mussorgsky (Mussorgsky)
5 *Katerina Izmaylova* (Shostakovich)
6 Last castrato (castrato; 20th-century music – chronology)
7 Purcell (Purcell)
8 Puccini (Puccini – caption)
9 *opera buffa* (opera)
10 Marie Antoinette (Gluck)

1 Wren (wren)
2 Heinkel (Heinkel, Ernst; flight)
3 Howard Hughes (Hughes, Howard)
4 Hovercraft (hovercraft)
5 Balance (wings)
6 Icarus (Icarus)
7 Igor Sikorsky (helicopter; Sikorsky)
8 Hawker (Harrier)
9 Rotor provides only lift and not propulsion (autogiro)
10 Leonard Cheshire (Cheshire)

1 Medea (Medea)
2 Margrethe II (Denmark – panel)
3 Laois (Laois)
4 She was stopped from entering the Abbey (Caroline of Brunswick)
5 Catherine de' Medici (Catherine de' Medici)
6 Maria Theresa (Maria Theresa)
7 Maud (Antarctica – map)
8 Tonga (Tonga)
9 Hatshepsut (Hatshepsut)
10 George Macdonald (Macdonald, George)

1 Heather (ling)
2 Methane (marsh gas)
3 Short sight (myopia)
4 Vitamin B_1 (thiamine)
5 Mother-of-pearl (nacre)
6 An oak tree (oak)
7 North Star (Polaris)
8 Magic mushroom (*Psilocybe*)
9 Blackcurrant (blackcurrant)
10 Raven (raven)

141   1990s

1 Imola (Senna)
2 Noureddine Morceli (Morceli)
3 Catamaran (sea transport – panel)
4 Jonathan Demme (Academy Awards – panel)
5 Rumbelows Cup (football, association)
6 James Stirling (Stirling, James)
7 Laos (Laos – panel)
8 Harrison Birtwistle (Birtwistle)
9 It was powered by flapping wings (flight – chronology)
10 Martin Amis (Amis, Martin)

142   Wars and Battles

1 American Civil War (Crane, Stephen)
2 George Patton (Patton – quote)
3 Cervantes (Lepanto, Battle of)
4 Boers (South African Wars)
5 Sir Walter Scott (Roses, Wars of the)
6 Yorktown, Virginia (American Revolution – chronology)
7 Russia (Russo-Japanese War)
8 Edward III (Crécy, Battle of)
9 Hell (Sherman – quote)
10 Tank (tank)

143   Human Body

1 In the thymus (thymus)
2 Factor VIII (haemophilia)
3 Oxygen (human body)
4 In the ovaries (oestrogen)
5 Ear (ear)
6 206 (skeleton)
7 In the foot (skeleton)
8 Parkinson's disease (dopamine)
9 In the inner ear (ear)
10 Melanin (melanism)

144   Kids' Stuff

1 14 (Education – chronology)
2 Britten (Britten)
3 Tutankhamen (Tutankhamen)
4 Maria Montessori (Montessori)
5 Narnia (Lewis, C S)
6 Richard III (Edward V)
7 Winnie-the-Pooh (Shepard – caption)
8 Uganda (Uganda Martyrs)
9 Brendan Behan (Behan)
10 Clarence Darrow (Darrow – quote)

145   Colours

1 Grey eminence (*éminence grise*)
2 Tintoretto (Tintoretto)
3 Westerns (Grey, Zane)
4 Alice Walker (Walker, Alice)
5 Ecology Party (Green Party)
6 Australia (wattle)
7 Red (Petra)
8 Carotene (carotene)
9 Uruguay (Uruguay)
10 Red (star)

146   Modern Scientists

1 That it gives off radio waves (Jansky)
2 Joule (Joule)
3 Roy Plunkett (Teflon)
4 Kelvin (Kelvin)
5 Thomas Young (corpuscular theory)
6 Fritz Haber (Haber process)
7 Hans Krebs (Krebs)
8 Peter Medawar (Medawar)
9 Barbara McClintock (gene)
10 Nature (Niepce)

147   Exiles and Emigrés

1 Alexander Solzhenitsyn (Solzhenitsyn)
2 Hawaii (Marcos)
3 Italy (Byron)
4 1964 (Khomeini)
5 Albert Einstein (Einstein)
6 Giuseppe Mazzini (Mazzini)
7 Charlie Chaplin (Chaplin)
8 Robert Louis Stevenson (Stevenson, Robert Louis)
9 Jimi Hendrix (Hendrix)
10 David Hockney (Hockney)

148   Discovery and Invention

1 The first asteroid (Ceres; Piazzi)
2 Frank Whittle (Whittle)
3 Laser (laser)
4 Ireland (railway – chronology)
5 John Hadley (sextant)
6 Electrons (electron; Thomson, J J)
7 Galileo (Galileo)
8 Machu Picchu (Machu Picchu)
9 Faraday (electromagnetic induction; Faraday)
10 The microscope (Leeuwenhoek; microscope)

149   Marks and Signs

1 Stations of the Cross (stations of the Cross)
2 Runes (rune)
3 A letter R (Rwanda – panel)
4 They cut themselves with knives (dervish)
5 Cecil B de Mille (de Mille, Cecil)
6 Paul Verlaine (Verlaine)
7 Black and yellow (beetle)
8 A winged dagger (Special Air Service)
9 Tarot (tarot cards)
10 They wore long trousers (sans-culotte)

150   Space: the Final Frontier

1 1664 (Jupiter)
2 8 (Neptune)
3 Ganymede (satellite – panel)
4 Mars (planets – panel)
5 Pluto (planets – panel)
6 Radio waves (quasar)
7 July (Armstrong, Neil)
8 Betelgeuse (Betelgeuse)
9 Hydrogen and helium (planets – panel)
10 Spiral (Milky Way)